Upgrade Your
Curriculum

Upgrade Your Curriculum

Practical Ways to Transform Units and Engage Students

Janet A. Hale
Michael Fisher

Foreword by Heidi Hayes Jacobs
Editor of *Curriculum 21*

1703 N. Beauregard St. • Alexandria, VA 22311-1714 USA
Phone: 800-933-2723 or 703-578-9600 • Fax: 703-575-5400
Website: www.ascd.org • E-mail: member@ascd.org
Author guidelines: www.ascd.org/write

Gene R. Carter, *Executive Director;* Mary Catherine (MC) Desrosiers, *Chief Program Development Officer;* Richard Papale, *Publisher;* Laura Lawson, *Acquisitions Editor;* Julie Houtz, *Director, Book Editing & Production;* Miriam Goldstein, *Editor;* Dayna Elefant, *Senior Graphic Designer;* Mike Kalyan, *Production Manager;* Cynthia Stock, *Typesetter;* Andrea Wilson, *Production Specialist*

Printed in the United States of America. Cover art © 2013 by ASCD. ASCD publications present a variety of viewpoints. The views expressed or implied in this book should not be interpreted as official positions of the Association.

All web links in this book are correct as of the publication date below but may have become inactive or otherwise modified since that time. If you notice a deactivated or changed link, please e-mail books@ascd.org with the words "Link Update" in the subject line. In your message, please specify the web link, the book title, and the page number on which the link appears.

PAPERBACK ISBN: 978-1-4166-1490-6   ASCD product #112014   n3/13
Also available as an e-book (see Books in Print for the ISBNs).

Quantity discounts: 10–49 copies, 10%; 50+ copies, 15%; for 1,000 or more copies, call 800-933-2723, ext. 5634, or 703-575-5634. For desk copies: www.ascd.org/deskcopy.

Library of Congress Cataloging-in-Publication Data

Hale, Janet A.
     Upgrade your curriculum : practical ways to transform units and engage students / Janet A. Hale and Michael Fisher.
          pages cm
     Includes bibliographical references and index.
     ISBN 978-1-4166-1490-6 (pbk. : alk. paper)
     1. Education—Curricula—United States. 2. Curriculum change—United States. 3. Curriculum planning—United States. I. Title.
     LB1570.H256 2013
     375'.001—dc23
                                                                                        2012043844

22 21 20 19 18 17 16 15 14 13   1 2 3 4 5 6 7 8 9 10 11 12

Janet Hale

I dedicate this book to Valerie Lyle.

Thank you for always believing in me,

inspiring me,

challenging me,

transforming me,

and being BFE (Best Friends Eternally).

Michael Fisher

I dedicate this book to Lily and Charlotte, my daughters.

I love that you are already curious, creative, and willing learners.

I am so proud of you both and look forward to the great experiences

we will get to share on your educational journey.

The world is your classroom.

Upgrade Your
Curriculum

Practical Ways to Transform Units and Engage Students

Acknowledgments   ix

Foreword   xi

Introduction   1

Part 1: Transforming the Curriculum   **7**

   1. Transformational Perspectives   9

   2. Transformational Lenses   15

   3. Applications of Technology and Web-Based Tools   26

   4. The Transformation Spiral   40

Part 2: Transformational Snapshots   **47**

   5. Ten-Frame Mathematics   49

   6. Flat Stanley Podcast   61

   7. Talk Pals   69

   8. Microloans: A Glocal Impact   81

   9. Film Festival   91

   10. Social Justice Live!   105

   11. Science in the Cloud   116

   12. Pinterest Art Critiques   123

   13. Common Core State Standards Professional Development   134

Part 3: Transformational Reflections   **141**

   14. A High School Student's Perspective   143

   15. More Than Meets the Eye   148

Appendix: TECHformational Matrices   151

References   165

Index   168

About the Authors   174

Acknowledgments

We would like to thank those who helped us make this book possible:

Heidi Hayes Jacobs: Thank you for being an educational cornerstone. As you continue to create a strong foundation, we will continue to build, build, build!

Laura Lawson and Miriam Goldstein: Thank you for your assistance while we continually tweaked our early drafts. Your guidance and editing skills have strengthened our work.

Joe Anastasi, Jim Cunningham, Ann Flagg, Steve Fulton, Keeli Garceau, Nathan Gingras, Linda Harrington, Aidan Lindberg, David Maidens, Brian Scully, Emily Todd, Jody Vaillancourt, and Bernard Waugh: Thank you for sharing your transformations with the world and for your continued dedication to creating modern-learning environments.

Silvia Rosenthal Tolisano: Thank you for being a modern-learning visionary. Your tenacity continually drives us and inspires us.

Curriculum 21 faculty: We look forward to spending time with you on the porch, both virtually and in person!

Janet

Johnny Hale: It is amazing to think we said "I do" 30 years ago (Mark 10:8). It seems like it was yesterday. I love you with all my heart!

Mike Fisher: Thank you for taking a wild writing ride with me. (You can squirrel on me anytime now that our book is done!)

Valerie Lyle: Thank you for being a critical friend who D.E.A.R. chapter after chapter. Your comments and suggestions were always right on!

Greg Lind: Your wordsmith wisdom always guides me through the writing process.

Daniel Gilmore: I can't imagine writing now without speak selection. What a treasure you shared!

Michael

Liz, Lily, and Charlotte Fisher: I love you all so much and promise I will be off the computer in just five more minutes!

Janet Hale: Thank you for being the best of what a true collaborator is: a contributor, a reviser, an editor, a scorpion hunter, and a javelina spy.

Tim Ito and everyone on ASCD EDge: Our conversations and interactions made this book even better than we had originally intended. Thank you!

Steven Weber: Your conversations, contributions, and willingness to read and respond quickly during the writing process were invaluable.

Tim Hortons coffee: Couldn't have done it without you, my friend.

Foreword

In *Curriculum 21: Essential Education for a Changing World* (2010), I developed the phrase "upgrading curriculum" in the hope that each teacher in every school would formally agree to strategically replacing a dated unit with a new practice. I believe that Janet Hale and Mike Fisher have "upgraded" upgrading. They have taken this key concept and created a detailed set of implementation steps to ensure that the learning trajectory of our students goes sky-high into the future.

If schools are launching pads, then Hale and Fisher are asking us to take a hard look at the planned trajectory of teaching and learning. If we view curriculum and assessment choices as indicators of the direction in which our students are heading, most of us would have to agree that we are preparing them to travel back in time to the 20th century. I have found that most educators want to create contemporary learning experiences, but they need to know how and where to start. *Upgrade Your Curriculum: Practical Ways to Transform Units and Engage Students* is a powerful resource that will guide teachers, principals, professional developers, and district leaders in these efforts.

As active collaborators and imaginative practitioners, Hale and Fisher have served up a 21st century curriculum feast for readers who sit at their table. Through their collaborative efforts, they have both expanded and refined the menu for improving the classroom lives of students and teachers. The expansion is evidenced through engaging case studies (Hale and Fisher call them "transformational snapshots") that reflect how real educators in specific settings have modernized units of study. These examples are marvelously personal, not only because the authors' writing style is so accessible but also because these stories are authentic. Hale and Fisher are two of the most vibrant and committed educators I know. They draw from a wealth of professional development experiences in schools across the United States and overseas. I have no doubt that the details of each snapshot will ring true, whether that snapshot focuses on enlivening a social justice unit, engaging primary-level learners with Flat Stanley gone global, or giving a math teacher a set of ten-frames to deepen students' understanding. A key feature of the snapshots is their creative applications of digital and media tools, thoughtfully organized based on a planning process that leads us to appraise and brainstorm, commit and communicate, react and reflect, and revise.

In addition to expanding the menu, the authors have also refined it. This refinement is evident in what I believe will prove a touchstone to the field: their *transformational matrix*. A dynamic and precise set of planning markers, this model provides a professional handrail to hold onto as we make the challenging transition from past practice to new versions of schooling. The matrix is timely given that we are in the midst of a confluence of messages regarding accountability, the Common Core State Standards, teacher effectiveness, and student performance. Yet overarching all these messages is the reality that we are now in the second decade of a new century that is requiring us to collectively step up curriculum in terms of both learning and teaching. Making this transition is daunting, and our schools need help in becoming contemporary institutions. It is reassuring to have this book in our hands and on our tablets.

On a personal level, it is a privilege to call Janet and Mike my colleagues and my friends. They are highly respected members of our Curriculum 21 faculty and can always be called on to step up and assist another teammate at the drop of a hat. Their work ethic is consistently rigorous, their sincere commitment to students is unquestionable, and their love of our work is contagious. I continue to learn from each of them as individuals, but in this foreword I want to particularly honor their collaboration. As you read this book, you will see how strongly they believe in communication and networking among professionals as crucial to quality transformation. In these pages, they have worked together to model what they preach through this dynamic and exciting opportunity to *upgrade your curriculum*.

Heidi Hayes Jacobs
The Curriculum 21 Project
www.curriculum21.com

Introduction

Alone we can do so little; together we can do so much.

—Helen Keller

Have you ever had a chance meeting with someone who ended up dramatically influencing your life? This was the case with us. Janet was hired to aid a district in its curriculum mapping initiative. Mike was working for a local educational service center and had been asked to attend the district training day as a technology specialist for the district's mapping software.

> **Janet:** During lunch, a few teachers and administrators, Mike, and I sat around a table and discussed everything from educational issues and current events to favorite movies and childhood experiences. I found Mike knowledgeable regardless of the topic, but most of all, I found him funny. He told a childhood story that literally made me laugh out loud.

> **Mike:** When I first met Janet on the training day, I had been involved in curriculum mapping initiatives, but I primarily focused on the technology. Honestly, I felt intimidated by her knowledge of mapping. I had no idea at the time that she felt intimidated by my knowledge of technology and web-based tools.

About two weeks after the training day, I (Janet) read an online cartoon that reminded me of Mike's humorous childhood memoir. I e-mailed the cartoon to

Mike, and our friendship began. We started e-mailing each other frequently for educational purposes. We discussed curriculum mapping, standards-based learning, instructional practices, and educational news. We began to co-present at various conferences, including ASCD's Annual Conference and the Curriculum Mapping Institute sponsored by Heidi Hayes Jacobs and Curriculum 21 (www.curriculum21.com).

We discovered over time that we enjoyed similar television shows and movies. When Disney released the movie *Up*, we quickly identified with two of the main characters: Carl and Dug. Carl, an elderly gentleman who can be a bit of a curmudgeon, is set in his ways and likes his routines. Dug is a dog who is valuable when accomplishing a task but often "squirrels," or gets off track easily. We decided that Janet is Carl and Mike is Dug. We can joke in this manner because over time we have become aware of our respective strengths and weaknesses and have used this knowledge to create a healthy partnership.

Our movie character metaphor reminds us that a healthy working relationship is built on mutual trust and respect and the ability to be vulnerable and depend on each other. Our collaboration in writing this book has further solidified our friendship and made us stronger as professionals.

We are sharing this information with you because collaboration is crucial in the 21st century. The Common Core State Standards (CCSS) clearly lay out the expectation that students must become proficient collaborators during their educational journeys, from their formative years to college and the workplace (National Governors Association Center for Best Practices [NGA Center] & Council of Chief State School Officers [CCSSO], 2010a). It follows that everyone involved in creating modern-learning environments for our current and future generations must participate in collaborative efforts.

In this book, we explain how teachers and administrators can upgrade their schools' current curriculum and recalibrate instructional practices to embrace modern learning. In modern-learning environments, students participate collaboratively in higher-order thinking tasks that often make local and global connections (and glocal impacts—more on these later) and include appropriate technology and web-based tools. We provide descriptions of the collaborative transformational process and in-the-field classroom experiences as well as specific strategies that emphasize student engagement and ownership of learning.

The seeds of *Upgrade Your Curriculum* are rooted deeply in Heidi Hayes Jacobs's *Curriculum 21* (2010). Jacobs explains:

> New essential curriculum will need revision—actual replacements of dated content, skills, and assessments with more timely choices. The steps and strategies presented here can focus a faculty on *upgrading* specific elements of the existing curriculum with more engaging and powerful selections. It is a nonthreatening approach that can be worked into the school culture gradually. Rather than a change model, it is a growth model. (pp. 12–13, italics added)

The upgrade concepts shared throughout *Curriculum 21* caused us to expand our personal and collaborative work to empower and enable teachers to successfully upgrade, or transform, units of study. We articulate specifics related to Jacobs's upgrading concepts throughout Part 1. In Chapter 3, we share the 21st Century Pledge that Jacobs created with teachers who were embarking on their upgrading journey.

We based *Upgrade Your Curriculum* on the premise that moving from *me* to *we* is an ongoing and essential process. Slow-and-steady upgrades or transformations, in which teachers (and students) work collaboratively to make strategic and specific modifications to current curricular elements, lead to modern, meaningful, and engaging experiences. We have found that once a collaborative culture is in place, participating in curriculum transformation continues to have positive effects on both teachers and students.

Book Overview

Part 1 of this book addresses the foundational concepts involved in transforming current curriculum for modern-learning environments. These four chapters explain the transformational matrix and its four zones, the five transformational lenses educators should use to focus on curriculum design, ways to purposefully and authentically incorporate technology and web-based tools into the curriculum, and the four phases of the transformational process.

Part 2 shows how various practitioners have used the transformational process to upgrade their curriculum and instructional practices. The nine narratives in these chapters include a range of grade levels and subject areas. The following list classifies each narrative, or *snapshot*, by school level:

Elementary School

Chapter 5: Ten-Frame Mathematics

Chapter 6: Flat Stanley Podcast

Chapter 7: Talk Pals

Middle School

Chapter 8: Microloans: A Glocal Impact

Chapter 9: Film Festival

Chapter 10: Social Justice Live!

High School

Chapter 11: Science in the Cloud

Chapter 12: Pinterest Art Critiques

Administration

Chapter 13: Common Core State Standards

Professional Development

Whichever your own subject area or grade level, we recommend reading all nine snapshots to get a full picture of the collaborative transformation of units of study. Each transformational snapshot includes three discussion questions to spark conversation among you and your colleagues.

The two short chapters in Part 3 consist of our own reflections—Janet's in Chapter 14 and Mike's in Chapter 15.

Finally, the Appendix includes 12 *TECHformational matrices*, or visual aids to be used as conversation starters by teachers and administrators as they consider potential technology-based transformations. Whereas the transformational matrix described in Chapter 1 focuses on overall student learning and engagement, the TECHformational matrices focus specifically on technology and web-based tools' potential to increase student engagement and ownership of learning. We have divided the TECHformational matrices into three categories: digital devices, web-based tools, and curations.

ASCD EDge

If you would like to be globally connected with those who are reading (or who have read) *Upgrade Your Curriculum,* plan to join us in our digital learning network on ASCD EDge (edge.ascd.org). We look forward to continuing to grow along with educators around the world as we share thoughts about the book's content, discuss the questions posed at the end of the chapters, and explore transformational snapshots submitted by practitioners, as we informate and amplify our collective thoughts and ideas.

Part I

Transforming the
Curriculum

We are now at a point where we must educate our children in what no one knew yesterday, and prepare our schools for what no one knows yet.

—Margaret Mead

Margaret Mead, a distinguished anthropologist, made the comment above in the mid-1950s. Her perceptions were, and still are, timely. It is estimated that by the year 2020, there will be 123 million high-paying, high-skill jobs in the United States, but only 50 million Americans will be capable of filling these positions (Winfrey, 2010). The key way to prove this prediction wrong is to provide students with meaningful units of study that mirror modern learning. The chapters in Part 1 address the foundational concepts involved in transforming current curriculum to accord with modern-learning environments.

Transformational Perspectives

Chapter 1 focuses on the necessity of professional collaboration in transforming units of study and explains the use of orbits of ability and digital learning networks. This chapter also introduces the transformational matrix and its four upgrade zones.

Transformational Lenses

Chapter 2 examines curriculum design and instructional practices as they relate to upgrading units of study through the lenses of teacher roles, entry levels, entry points, 21st century clarifications, and standards connections.

Applications of Technology and Web-Based Tools

Chapter 3 discusses the authentic incorporation of technology and web-based tools in modern-learning environments and explains the purpose and use of the TECH-formational matrices included in the Appendix.

The Transformation Spiral

Chapter 4 provides an overview of the transformation spiral's four phases: appraisal and brainstorming, commitment and communication, reactions and reflections, and revisions.

1

Transformational Perspectives

*Working with you . . . allowed this movie to be the
truest version of what it would be.*

—J. J. Abrams

J. J. Abrams's observation (Jensen, 2011) about his collaboration with Steven Spielberg on their film *Super 8* encapsulates what transforming curriculum involves: collaborating to create a curriculum that exceeds the originally planned version. Collaboration is not new. But in 21st century classrooms, there are new expectations for what collaborations should entail and aim toward.

Educators who design curriculum exemplify these new expectations. A curriculum map, a single unit of study, or a detailed instructional plan is the result of collaborative and collegial conversations and decision making (Hale & Dunlap, 2010). Teachers must ask hard questions based on their interpretation of standards, determination of big ideas and essential questions, and development of authentic performance tasks, all the while respecting others' thoughts and ideas, negotiating what to cut and what to keep (and why), and determining what is in students' best interests.

This chapter lays a foundation on which the next three chapters build, explaining what teachers need to do as they begin the collaborative process of upgrading curriculum one unit at a time. To create modern-learning environments, educators cannot function as if they are preparing students for 1982 (Jacobs, 2010). When teachers begin transforming curriculum, they must

• Actively seek out collaborative relationships (orbits of ability) that facilitate the process of upgrading units of study.

• Consider how each of the four main categories of upgrading units of study affects student learning and engagement.

Orbits of Ability

A teacher who aims to transform curriculum must first consider which *orbits of ability* are necessary to upgrade a particular unit of study. An *orbit of ability* is a given person's knowledge and talent, or expertise. When one person moves into another person's orbit of ability, his or her knowledge and capabilities grow (see Figure 1.1). Every teacher has his or her own orbit or orbits of ability that others can learn from. Accessing orbits of ability can take place during any interaction with colleagues, friends, family members, or even a new acquaintance.

The most effective way for teachers to ensure that their orbits' edges touch is to work together purposefully to improve one another's capabilities. The more orbits of ability that overlap, the greater the degree of professional growth. As the isolated orbit in Figure 1.1 demonstrates, a person may have an expertise that he or she is not willing to share. In modern-learning (and modern-teaching) environments,

---

FIGURE

1.1 Orbits of Ability

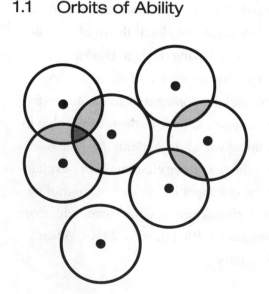

Orbit of Ability

Orbit Edges Touching =
Personal Growth

Orbit Overlap (Shaded Area) =
Collaborative Growth

someone who chooses not to share his or her expertise will eventually have difficulty functioning in the workplace.

During the curriculum transformation process, it is imperative that participants feel comfortable admitting when they do not know necessary information or lack certain abilities. Teachers must be given social and emotional permission to be learners with their colleagues and administrators. The teachers responsible for transforming a unit of study need to seek out the people whose orbits of ability are required to upgrade the unit. These experts will vary depending on the unit's content, task, and purpose. The transformational snapshots in Part 2 provide nine examples of educators seeking out orbits of ability to aid them in upgrading their units of study.

Digital Learning Networks

Active participation in a well-functioning professional learning community (PLC) has proven to help improve student learning (DuFour, Eaker, & DuFour, 2005). This is true for those involved in Internet-based collaborations as well. Educators can connect and interact online with fellow educators through *digital learning networks* (DLNs) using social networking tools such as Facebook, Twitter, Diigo, and ASCD EDge (edge.ascd.org). If your school site or district filters social networking sites, consider using a personal computer or device to network after school hours until Internet access policies change.

In the 21st century, geographical location has become inconsequential to networking, sharing, collaborating, organizing, and creating. The Common Core State Standards for English Language Arts and Literacy (NGA Center & CCSSO, 2010a) expect modern classrooms to emulate students' eventual workplace settings, "in which people from often widely divergent cultures and who represent diverse experiences and perspectives must learn and work together" (p. 7). If we want our students to one day be able to learn and work with colleagues from widely divergent cultures, we must model these expectations in the educational workplace. Educators need to communicate effectively with others for specific tasks and purposes, evaluate others' points of view constructively and respectfully, and collaboratively transform professional practice using technology and web-based tools strategically and capably.

Active networking through DLNs increases teachers' access to orbits of ability when they are brainstorming or planning an upgraded unit of study. For example, a small group of teachers working with an instructional coach we know asked the coach to help them brainstorm alternatives to having their students create a traditional diorama. The instructional coach immediately logged in to her Twitter account using her mobile device and sent a tweet to inquire whether anyone had any innovative alternative ideas. Within minutes, multiple responses appeared that provided a wide variety of suggestions and links to resources. The instructional coach and the group of teachers immediately used this instantaneous information to develop a wiki at www.wikispaces.com.

Linda Darling-Hammond (1997) reminds educators that "the challenge of ensuring success for all students requires teachers and school leaders to work and learn collaboratively, reflect on their practice, and continually expand their knowledge and skills" (p. 15). Getting involved in DLNs is one way to rise to the challenge of collaborating professionally and expanding our knowledge and understanding.

The Transformational Matrix

Whether you collaborate on curriculum transformation in person or virtually, it is helpful to have a visual reference that represents the four categories of potential upgrade, or *upgrade zones*. The transformational matrix (see Figure 1.2) classifies these upgrade zones according to the degree of their impact on student learning and engagement.

The transformational matrix is not meant to convey that the outcomes of an upgraded unit of study are neat and clean and fit perfectly into one of four boxes. When teachers are asked, "What constitutes a positive impact on learning and engagement?" answers will vary depending on teachers' personal and professional experiences as well as on the school or district's collaboration history and current culture. Here is what each upgrade zone looks like in action:

• **Conform** (low impact on learning/low impact on engagement). In this zone, the actions of teachers are more visible than are those of students. Even when teachers include technology and web-based tools in the unit of study, students are passive receptors of the content.

• **Outform** (low impact on learning/high impact on engagement). In this zone, the purposeful use of technology and web-based tools increases student engagement, but the transformation is largely aesthetic. Interactions in this zone are sometimes referred to as "playground experiences," because the students are

FIGURE

1.2 Transformational Matrix

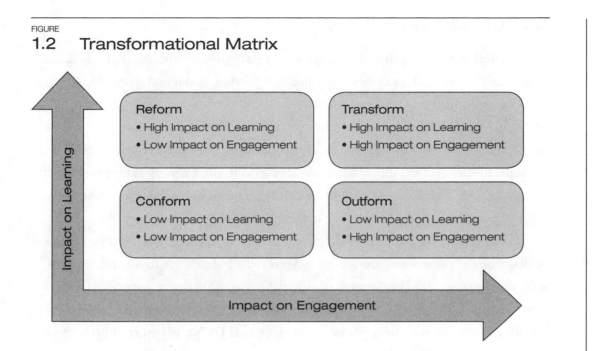

active and engaged in the learning process. Closer examination, however, reveals that students' contributions to their learning process are based on what the teacher has selected or created.

• **Reform** (high impact on learning/low impact on engagement). In this zone, students' interactions are based on an articulated task and purpose. The teacher may or may not be the audience. Students create content rather than simply react to what the teacher has created or selected. This zone tends to generate greater student achievement but may not necessarily be engaging for students. Cognitive and metacognitive expectations require deeper thinking and justification but could be accomplished without technology or web-based tools, although they are incorporated into a unit of study.

• **Transform** (high impact on learning/high impact on engagement). This zone represents student-centered ownership of learning. Students not only create content and choose software and web-based tools to use, but also make choices based on a specific task, purpose, and audience. The teacher acts as a facilitator for learning in this zone. Students engage in authentic higher-order thinking and often share their work and thoughts beyond the classroom walls using self-selected technology and web-based tools.

Discussion Questions

1. When explaining the transformational matrix, we mentioned that educators might have varying ideas of what constitutes a positive impact on student learning and engagement. How has your educational system encouraged teachers to collaboratively establish what cognitively and socially constitute positive impacts on student learning and engagement? If your school or district has not worked collectively to establish these expectations, what might you do to work through this process with your colleagues? How would your team come to consensus or calibrate the definitions of positive impacts on learning and engagement?

2. You can access orbits of ability in person or virtually. How would you define or describe the talents and knowledge in your personal orbit or in others' orbits of ability? If you are not comfortable with social networking or the concept of DLNs, whose orbit of ability could you access for assistance? If your own orbit of ability includes a comfort with using social networking and DLNs, whom could you assist in establishing their own DLNs?

3. The transformational matrix's vertical and horizontal arrows purposefully do not read "Positive Impact on Learning" because educators' interpretations of *positive* could vary. How does the explanation of each upgrade zone shape your understanding of what the four zones constitute?

2

Transformational Lenses

To me, eyewear goes way beyond being a prescription. . . . The shape of a frame or the color of lenses can change your whole appearance.

—Vera Wang

Although Vera Wang was talking about glasses, her observations apply to more than eyewear. Just as changing your glasses can change your whole appearance, upgrading certain aspects of a unit of study can change the unit's entire appearance. Student-centered, 21st century units of study help develop independent and interdependent critical thinkers, creative problem solvers, collaborators, communicators, and contributors. As Stewart (2012) observes, educators must focus on curriculum design and instructional practice with a 21st century mind-set:

> We all have a tendency to think that the curriculum that was in place when we went to school ought to be the curriculum of today. This is comfortable for everyone—teachers, academic experts, and parents. But just as the 19th century school curriculum of the agricultural era gave way to a more scientific and technical curriculum after the industrial revolution (Zhao, 2009), so the hyperdigital and global world of the 21st century will demand different knowledge and skills from our students if they are to be successful. . . . The world is changing at breakneck speed. How can we, as educators, best prepare our students for the jobs of the future, many of which have not even been invented yet? What will our students need to be successful citizens and leaders not only in their own communities but in the nation and the world? (pp. 122–123)

15

This chapter highlights five transformational lenses that are important for educators to keep in focus as they strategically transform units of study and update instructional approaches for the 21st century. These lenses include

- Teacher roles.
- Entry levels.
- Entry points.
- 21st century clarifications.
- Standards connections.

Teacher Roles: Architect and Contractor

Although there is a symbiotic relationship between learning and teaching, *learning* focuses on curriculum design while *teaching* focuses on instructional practice (Hale & Dunlap, 2010). Because teachers are not often asked to be curriculum designers unless they are involved in curriculum mapping or a specialized master's or doctorate program, they may initially find it difficult to differentiate between curriculum design and instructional practice. It is helpful to think of a metaphor commonly used by experts in the education field: teachers need to be both *architects* and *contractors* (Jacobs, 2002).

Architects design blueprints; teachers design curriculum. Like architects, teachers must first consider building codes (standards); the structure's function (e.g., enduring understandings, essential questions, unit/supporting questions, and concepts); and the form based on the structure's function (content, skills, assessments, and evaluations). Architects design blueprints using words and symbols that enable other architects and contractors to interpret what the expectations are during and after construction.

Contractors build according to blueprints; teachers instruct according to designed curriculum. Teacher-architects who create curriculum or are involved in curriculum mapping need to switch roles and become teacher-contractors. In this role, they collaboratively and individually make decisions on how to sequence the construction (e.g., instructional practices) while staying in close contact with the building's future residents (e.g., differentiating instruction for students); keeping in mind the building-code requirements related to the function and form (the standards); and adjusting construction as needed based on periodic inspections (e.g., formative assessments, evaluations, and feedback).

Entry Levels

Transforming curriculum asks teachers to actively and collaboratively take on two roles: designing 21st century curriculum and incorporating 21st century instructional practices. The process of upgrading units of study may require teachers to modernize learning (curriculum design), teaching (instructional practice), or a combination of the two. There are three possible *entry levels*—places to begin the transformational process—when transforming curriculum:

- A unit of study (*learning* expectations).
- A unit of study's instructional plan (strategic overview of *teaching* based on the unit's *learning* expectations).
- A series of lessons that support the instructional plan (specific details for *teaching* the unit's *learning* expectations).

Whichever entry level teachers formally select, the changes they make to it will often affect other entry levels too. Whichever the entry level targeted, the goal is the same: to replace dated learning or teaching practices. Jacobs (2010) challenges teachers as curriculum designers and instructional practitioners to help students become full-time residents of the 21st century:

> Our questions will be straightforward: What do we cut? What do we keep? What do we create? . . . Our goal as authors is to stimulate specific dialogue, specific debate, and specific actions for your considerations at all levels. . . . We invite your engagement into Curriculum 21. (pp. 2, 4)

Entry Points

While teachers consider entry levels for a particular unit of study, they must simultaneously select one or more *entry points*, or aspects of one or more entry levels where upgrades could potentially take place. Teachers upgrading units of study commonly use the entry points we discuss in the following sections. In these sections, we provide information to illuminate aspects of the entry points that might affect your decisions on curriculum design and instructional practice during the transformational process.

Performance Task Assessments

What makes tasks and assessments authentic? An Olympic athlete practices to meet a unique challenge in a demonstration of his or her athletic skills. A job interviewee needs to prove his or her value in conversation and possibly through a demonstration of his or her abilities. How many multiple-choice tests are able to prove a person's capabilities in a professional setting?

Authenticity plays a pivotal role in modernizing assessments. According to Wiggins and McTighe (2005), "to get evidence of true understanding requires that we elicit learner judgments made during genuine performance, not just seeing how they respond to easily followed cues that require mere recall and plugging in" (p. 155). For performance task assessments to have genuine value, the teacher's instructional practices must help develop the task's intentions. A project-based, problem-based, or performance-based unit's intent is for students to collaboratively solve a real-world problem or investigate why phenomena occur. For a problem-solving unit, the performance task assessment should have students collaboratively reach a research-based solution for an intended audience. For a phenomenon-oriented unit, students need to work together to curate information—that is, select the information that they decide is the most relevant based on the unit's task and purpose—and present it to an intended audience. Students may share their results in person or virtually, using technology and web-based tools.

Edutopia (2011) provides 10 tips for assessing project-based learning. Although some of the tips focus on what teachers should be doing, the first tip focuses on what students need to be able to do:

> Students . . . learn more deeply by doing—or that's the goal at least. . . . If you've relied on traditional tests for assessment in the past, now's your chance to think outside the (check) box to find more-authentic ways for students to demonstrate what they know and are able to do. Over the course of a project, students might take on the roles of scientists, historians, screenwriters, or experts from other disciplines. Look to these disciplines for appropriate end-of-project assessment ideas. What sorts of products would you expect from a biologist, poet, or social scientist? What do professionals from these fields make, do, or perform? Expect similar products or performances from your students at the culmination of a project to show what they have learned. Authentic products naturally reflect the learning goals and content standards you have identified during project planning. They don't feel fake or forced. . . . For example, students in Maine created an activity book about oceans to interest and entertain young diners at a waterfront restaurant. Compelling research presentations by students in Rochester, New York, convinced the city council to invest in a feasibility study about restoring a historic waterway. . . . Sharing their final products with an audience brings students valuable feedback and an opportunity to reflect on what they have learned. (p. 3).

Keep in mind that a performance task assessment is most often the summation of a unit. Throughout the unit, the teacher should provide continual feedback and formative assessments to enable students to execute the ultimate performance assessment.

Culminating Experiences

You probably have memories, personal or professional, of a time when education readily afforded students opportunities to participate in ungraded, unevaluated experiences. We often retain affectionate memories of these school experiences for a lifetime.

In our current education climate of accountability and high-stakes testing, we still need to carve out time to provide memory-making experiences for children and young adults. Project-based or problem-based units can be time-consuming. If a school or district requires teachers to focus intensely on specific content and skills, teachers can still upgrade the unit by having students participate in an event that celebrates their learning. These culminating experiences are not meant to be graded or intensely evaluated; they are meant to be enjoyed.

For example, the Flat Stanley Podcast project we describe in Chapter 6 incorporated a culminating experience. Although students were graded on their work throughout the unit, the culminating experience of publishing their podcast on the Internet was an opportunity to celebrate what they had accomplished.

Curriculum Examinations

Curriculum design audits and curriculum revision cycles have been in place in most states, districts, and schools for many years. The problem is that audits or revisions do not always take place as often as they need to. Some schools may not revise a given discipline's curriculum for over a decade. Fortunately, this practice is changing, and many districts and schools are now conducting curriculum examinations in a timely manner.

There are times when teachers systematically examine the current curriculum by conducting reviews and revising the learning according to academic standards or other criteria. In other kinds of curriculum review, teachers examine a particular unit of study to determine areas that need revision or upgrading through the cutting or addition of content, skills, concepts, or understandings (Jacobs, 2010). As Jacobs (2011) observed in a curriculum mapping keynote presentation, "Teachers are doctors. Students are patients in their care. Curriculum maps, instructional plans, and lessons are prescriptions. It is important that what is being prescribed is in the patients' best interests."

Along with determining what to cut, keep, or create, teachers need to focus on authentically integrating technology and web-based tools, which we address in detail in Chapter 3. Today's learners are plugged into a technological world that is growing exponentially, and they will not unplug for the sake of learning content that does not matter to them. Likewise, they do not want to be part of yesterday's instructional system. To put today's technological world into context, consider what takes place within a 60-second period on the Internet. According to Go-Gulf (2011), every 60 seconds,

- 600 videos are uploaded on YouTube, which amounts to more than 25 hours of content.
- 695,000 status updates, 79,364 wall posts, and 510,040 comments are published on Facebook.
- 320 new accounts and 98,000 tweets are generated on Twitter.
- iPhone applications are downloaded more than 13,000 times.
- 370,000+ minutes of voice calls are initiated by Skype users.
- 1,600+ reads are made on Scribd, the world's largest social reading and publishing company.

Now consider that your students are likely participating in these happenings—possibly during school hours.

Instructional Innovations

We must take into account today's technological reality when we consider innovations to our instructional practices. Does our current classroom instruction mimic the real world? Jacobs (2010) elaborates:

> I often wonder if many of our students feel like they are time traveling as they walk through the school door each morning. As they cross the threshold, do they feel as if they are entering a simulation of life in the 1980s? Then, at the end of the school day, do they feel that they have returned to the 21st century? As educators, our challenge is to match the needs of our learners to a world that is changing with great rapidity. To meet this challenge, we need to become strategic learners ourselves by deliberately expanding our perspectives and updating our approaches. (p. 7)

Being a teacher in the 21st century does not mean what it did in previous decades (and centuries). A teacher no longer needs to be the most knowledgeable person in the room. Students enjoy being self-directed learners and need a strong "guide on the side" rather than a "sage on the stage."

A teacher's wisdom, expertise, and years of living on planet Earth are indispensable. In a modern-learning classroom, the teacher plays a critical and delicate role in allowing his or her students to explore and make sense of the world around them. Innovative teachers are willing to take risks and not just do what is familiar or has always worked in the past. There is great value and benefit when teachers are willing to be co-learners with those in their classrooms, to work alongside rather than always ahead of their students.

21st Century Clarifications

The common entry points we have discussed—performance task assessments, culminating experiences, curriculum examinations, and instructional innovations—involve four concepts that warrant clarification: higher-order thinking, collaborative environments, local and global connections, and glocal impacts. Although these concepts may be familiar, they take on added dimensions within the context of 21st century learning environments, which include technology authenticity related to potential upgrades.

Higher-Order Thinking

As teachers begin to shift their views on instructional innovations and rethink their classroom roles, they must take care to incorporate opportunities for students to engage in authentic higher-order thinking. Many teachers do not go beyond asking higher-order questions. Although there is a time and a place for such questioning, students should also be asking themselves and others questions that require deep thinking, and they must be able to provide logical reasoning for their answers and arguments. They must be choice makers, problem solvers, and creators. They should individually and collaboratively be able to

• Make choices about how to acquire necessary information (which could also include what needs to be learned in order to complete an authentic task).

• Discern relevant information while thinking critically about the task, purpose, and, possibly, audience for a given assignment or assessment.

• Solve authentic problems and share solutions with an authentic audience.

Because these requisites are at the core of preparedness for 21st century college and careers, students need to learn to

- Think critically about the information they access.
- Discern credibility and intended meaning of the information they access.
- Reason fluently, both inductively and deductively.
- Make logical and thoughtful decisions based on collected, curated, and analyzed information.

Students also need opportunities to creatively solve problems involving interdisciplinary content and concepts that encourage them to actively obtain knowledge and understanding rather than be passive receptors (Jacobs, 2010; Wiggins & McTighe, 2011). In a student-centered classroom where authentic tasks provide opportunities for higher-order thinking, students' intrinsic motivation and desire to learn flourish (November, 2012).

Collaborative Environments

The Framework for 21st Century Learning developed by the Partnership for 21st Century Skills (2009) emphasizes that students must "demonstrate [the] ability to work effectively and respectfully with diverse teams" (p. 4).

Teachers have used collaboration as an instructional tool in their classrooms for years, having students work in pairs, triads, or small groups in such roles as facilitators, timekeepers, and recorders. Twenty-first century collaborative groupings include new roles, such as interviewers, bloggers, backchannel mediators, videographers, and data recorders. In addition, the concept of collaboration is no longer limited to a classroom's four walls. Videoconferencing with web-based tools such as Skype or ooVoo enables classrooms to make local and global connections with the click of a mouse. Students in the United States can interact, explore, or make presentations with students in Beijing, China; Frankfurt, Germany; and Rio de Janeiro, Brazil.

These new collaborative roles and capabilities will eventually become a ubiquitous component of modern-learning environments. Until then, teachers need to work diligently to embed these expectations purposefully in their upgraded units of study. For some teachers, this might mean reaching out to those whose orbits of ability include a comfort level with technology and web-based tools.

Local and Global Connections

Making virtual connections with people locally and globally is a natural component of 21st century collaborative environments. Technology and web-based tools now enable teachers and students to connect with people outside their immediate locations. Using Skype or other face-to-face virtual meeting forums brings learning alive in a way that was not possible just a few years ago. Students need to participate in two types of virtual connections:

• Local connections involve one class's interactions with another class within the same state or province.

• Global connections involve one class's interactions with another class outside the initiating class's state or province borderline.

To gain an authentic understanding of local and global peoples, their societies, and how they survive and thrive, students need to make purposeful local and global connections. Teachers also need to strategically prepare students for college and careers that might exist in unfamiliar or far-flung locations. Even close to home, diversity in the workplace is commonplace, so students need to understand others' cultures. There is no one way to design curriculum and instructional practice to prepare students for college and careers. Students in New York, New York, have different perspectives and understandings than students in New London, North Carolina, do. Although both New York and North Carolina have adopted the Common Core State Standards, the teacher-architects and teacher-contractors in these two locations need to consider the specific recipients of their respective curriculum blueprints.

Glocal Impacts

The term *glocal* is not a misprint or a typographical error. It combines the words *global* and *local* into one word with a specific meaning: acting locally to effect change for the better somewhere else in the world. It is important to note that this term applies even when the care recipients are within the state borders of the caregivers. In other words, students in Kansas City, Missouri, who raised money to send bottles of water to those struck by the horrific tornadoes in Joplin, Missouri, in May 2011 made a glocal impact. Likewise, a high school class that decides to solicit sponsorships for water-well construction in drought-stricken areas of Africa is also making a glocal impact.

Students who participate in a glocal-impact unit of study are engaged in interdisciplinary learning involving a local or global people's issues, beliefs, and heritage. Although there is often a specific discipline at the forefront of the unit's focus, the authentic nature of the unit enables students to experience how different disciplines intersect and connect. Glocal-impact units also require students to make collaborative decisions based on their research into the needs of those they are serving. The transformational snapshot in Chapter 8 ("Microloans: A Glocal Impact") describes a glocal-impact unit in which 8th grade students provided microloans to entrepreneurs living halfway around the world.

Standards Connections

Local, state, national, and international educational standards should never be viewed as static guidelines. Just as societies evolve based on what has been, what is, and what needs to be, standards focused on what learners need to know and be able to do will continue to evolve. When standards used to design students' learning are amended, revised, or presented anew, educators often express frustration. Teachers may think that all the effort they took to design standards-based curriculum maps and unit plans was a waste of time, but this is not true. Curriculum design is a continual work in progress.

Common Core State Standards: Capacities and Practices

The CCSS process-skills standards for both English language arts and mathematics explicitly and implicitly require students to become

- Higher-order thinkers.
- Collaborators.
- Performers of authentic tasks.
- Local and global connectors.
- Strategic and capable users of technology and web-based tools.

The process-skills standards provide meaningful and purposeful context for the CCSS content standards. Together, both sets of standards aim to prepare students for college and careers so that they can flourish in their professional endeavors and actively contribute to the livelihoods of future generations (Stewart, 2012).

When upgrading units of study based on the Common Core State Standards, teacher-architects must combine the content standards *and* the process-skills standards. Although the descriptions of the upgraded units of study in Part 2's transformational snapshots do not include specific content standards, the transformational lenses table within each chapter includes the Standards for Mathematical Practice or the English Language Arts College and Career Readiness (CCR) Capacities embedded in the transformed unit when appropriate.

A New Vision

The frameworks, models, and visionary ideas of forward thinkers like Heidi Hayes Jacobs, Grant Wiggins, Jay McTighe, Vivien Stewart, and Alan November aid teachers and students in creating 21st century learning and teaching. In his explanation of his *digital learning farm* model, November (2012) synthesizes the transformational lenses we have discussed in this chapter:

> The tools we have today can help us craft a new vision that empowers our students to own and lead more of their own learning. The goal of the digital learning farm model is to redefine the role of the learner as a contributor, collaborator, and leader in the learning culture. . . . Imagine a school where every learner is valued for making a contribution to benefit the whole class. The questions (1) Who owns the learning? and (2) Who works harder in the classroom, the teacher or the student? drive the thinking behind the solutions. (p. 6)

Discussion Questions

1. As you consider potential units of study in your school that you could upgrade based on the entry levels, entry points, and 21st century clarifications discussed in this chapter, which units come to mind, and why?

2. Although the terminology may be new, your community is probably already involved in making glocal impacts. Often, these occur as acts of kindness and are not intentionally tied in to school curriculum. Which units of study could you transform to incorporate glocal impacts?

3. Reread the quotation from November (2012) on this page and contemplate the two questions he poses. What would a unit of study look like academically/cognitively and collaboratively/socially if the students owned the learning and worked harder in the classroom?

3

Applications of Technology and Web-Based Tools

Man is still the most extraordinary computer of all.

—John F. Kennedy

In his book *Empowering Students with Technology*, Alan November (2010) describes a *Wall Street Journal* cartoon that depicts a student standing on top of a computer monitor to reach a high point on the chalkboard. The cartoon's message underscores a common misconception: that upgrading curriculum simply means incorporating technology—any technology.

In reality, upgrading curriculum involves the purposeful, task-oriented, and authentic use of

- **Technology hardware** (e.g., computers, LCD projectors, interactive whiteboards, response clickers, Flip cameras, document cameras).
- **Technology software** (e.g., word-processing programs, interactive games, applications downloaded to a phone, programs downloaded to a computer).
- **Web-based tools** (e.g., Google Docs, cloud-based organizational tools like LiveBinders).

In 21st century learning environments, students are expected to participate collaboratively in higher-order thinking tasks that often make local and global connections (and glocal impacts) and incorporate appropriate technology and web-based tools. The Common Core State Standards for English Language Arts require that students

[U]se technology and digital media strategically and capably. Students employ technology thoughtfully to enhance their reading, writing, speaking, listening, and language use. They tailor their searches online to acquire useful information efficiently, and they integrate what they learn using technology with what they learn offline. They are familiar with the strengths and limitations of various technological tools and mediums and can select and use those best suited to their communication goals. (NGA Center & CCSSO, 2010a, p. 7)

Automating, Informating, Amplifying

It is important for schools going through the process of creating modern-learning environments to distinguish curriculum *transformation* from mere *enhancement*. Enhancement represents an aesthetic change, whereas genuine transformation involves deeper change. The best way to understand the nuances of the two terms is to visualize them as opposite ends of a continuum, with the concepts of *automating, informating,* and *amplifying* representing gradations between the two terms (see Figure 3.1).

Automating

Automating is closest to the enhancement end of the continuum and refers to the use of technology that does not demand a significant change in instructional practice, assessment, or student thinking. Although an automating curriculum upgrade may appear to involve 21st century skills, its expectations of students are similar or equivalent to those in the traditional learning environment. In an automating environment, the teacher maintains control of both the learning and the teaching.

Stage 1: Substitution. The first stage of an automating upgrade is *substitution* (Hos-McGrane, 2010). A teacher who uses an interactive whiteboard to present a lesson that she previously presented on a chalkboard is merely substituting one delivery method for another; she is not changing the lesson's essential purpose or functionality. Similarly, a teacher who has students complete a multiple-choice test using response clickers rather than paper and pencil has made a *substitution automating* upgrade. The assessment itself demands the same cognition of students.

Rosenthal Tolisano (2011a) describes an example of a substitution upgrade of a traditional book report:

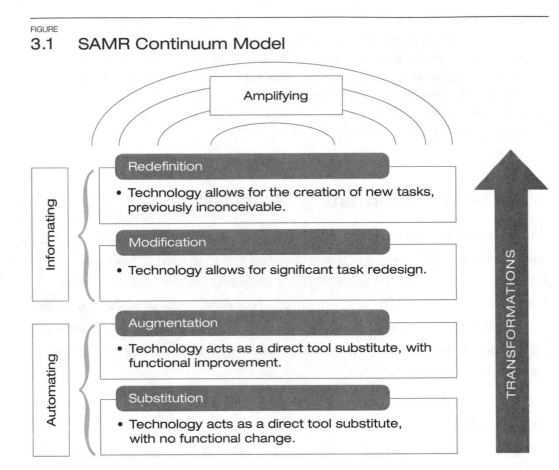

FIGURE
3.1   SAMR Continuum Model

Based on the SAMR Model by R. Puentedura (2011) built on ideas shared by A. November (2010). Visual adaptation by S. Rosenthal Tolisano (2011a).

Instead of having students handwrite the report, teachers are allowing them to type it up and print it out before handing it in. The teacher will then read it, mark spelling and grammar mistakes, point out possible omissions, grade it, and then hand it back to the students. Using the computer to type substituted (automated) the task of writing the report by hand. There was no functional change. . . . Students went through the same cognitive process as they were producing the report. (paras. 6–7)

A substitution upgrade correlates with the *conform* zone of the transformational matrix (see Figure 1.2, p. 13).

Stage 2: Augmentation. To move to the second automating stage, *augmentation,* a teacher needs to use technology that demands purposeful functionality (Hos-McGrane, 2010). An augmentation upgrade often increases the demand on students' cognitive or metacognitive skills. Rosenthal Tolisano (2011a) continues:

The student types the assigned book report and instead of printing it out and handing it in to the teacher the following school day uses Google Docs to "share" the file with her teacher. The teacher then enters comments on the Google Docs file. The student goes over the teacher's suggestions and edits the same document before a given deadline, when the teacher looks at the final edit and then grades the report.

In this scenario, the student's thinking process as she produced the book report did not change. Technology allowed her to *share* versus *hand in* the assignment, which added functionality to the process. (paras. 8–9)

An *augmentation* upgrade may correlate with the *conform* zone of the transformational matrix but could also correlate with the *outform* or *reform* zone, depending on the new degree of student cognition required.

Informating

Although using technology and web-based tools may improve the quality of instruction and its delivery, a truly upgraded unit of study must engage students as active participants in gathering, analyzing, evaluating, synthesizing, and creating information. November (2010) distinguishes *informating*, the middle gradation on the enhancement-transformation continuum, from *automating* in terms of student engagement and ownership:

Automating essentially means "bolting" technology on top of current processes and procedures. When an organization automates, the locus of control remains the same, the time and place remain the same, and the relationships remain the same. . . . Informating is a more powerful way of thinking about technology than automating. While informating can lead to a much higher-quality improvement, it is much more difficult to implement. It is not that the technology is more difficult to learn: in fact, very often an informated application uses the same technology as an automated one. What makes it more powerful is a shift of control and empowerment. (pp. 2–5)

An *informating* classroom includes four crucial elements:

• Students' learning is not sourced solely from information shared by the teacher.

• Students work collaboratively to obtain information (including facts, concepts, materials, and resources).

• Students synthesize the information they have collected and determine which information to use to complete the assigned task.

• Students use technology, software, and web-based tools to share their *curated*, or strategically selected and notated, information with the teacher and their classmates.

Stage 1: Modification. The first informating stage, *modification*, requires tasks themselves to be redesigned (Hos-McGrane, 2010). Rosenthal Tolisano (2011a) uses the same example of the book report to clarify:

> The teacher modifies the original task of writing about a book to go beyond paraphrasing and expanding the summary of the book sleeve. She asks her students to include research about the author, historic events during the author's writing of the book, timelines, and connections to other authors of the same genre or topic. The teacher encourages students to go beyond the traditional "research" sources, such as other books, newspaper articles, or journals and venture into sources such as Twitter, YouTube, Delicious, blogs, and Shelfari. . . . The teacher is teaching her students to take advantage of the tools in the information age, helping and guiding them to develop skills and information literacy. (paras. 10–11)

Stage 2: Redefinition. *Redefinition* is the second informating stage (Hos-McGrane, 2010). It requires students to select and use technology and web-based tools to complete a task in a way that was previously unavailable or unimaginable. (Note: For younger students, the teacher could present two or three options for students to select from.) Rosenthal Tolisano (2011a) extends the book report example to explain this stage:

> The teacher decides that students should not be confined to producing a book report in only one medium (text). She chooses to give students the freedom to use different media to create a summary of their chosen book, express their own interpretation based on research, and possibly add a recommendation for a specific audience (e.g., classmates) of why or why not to read the book. Students could create a PowerPoint presentation, a podcast, a video trailer, a multimedia poster, or another product. Students prepare their "reports" by researching, storyboarding, and searching for or producing their own media to create the final product.
>
> In this scenario, students are learning to express themselves and to communicate through different media. The task of thinking about a book and writing (in text) about its author, setting, characters, plot, and so on has been redesigned to include multiple media that demand different forms of expression and have different audiences. Without the use of technology and web-based tools, this task would not be possible. (paras. 12–13)

Living in the information age has enabled us to move from an *automating* teaching and learning environment to an *informating* environment. In a TEDx Talk, Laufenberg (2010) described the beginning of our evolution from information scarcity to information surplus:

In 1931, my grandmother . . . graduated from the 8th grade. She went to school to get the information because that's where the information lived. It was in the books; it was inside the teacher's head; and she needed to go there to get the information, because that's how you learned. Fast-forward a generation: this is the one-room schoolhouse, Oak Grove, where my father went. . . . And he again had to travel to the school to get the information from the teacher, stored it in the only portable memory he has, which is inside his own head, and take it with him, because that is how information was being transported from teacher to student and then used in the world. When I was a kid, we had a set of encyclopedias at my house. It was purchased the year I was born, and it was extraordinary, because I did not have to wait to go to the library to get to the information. The information was inside my house and it was awesome. This was different than either generation had experienced before, and it changed the way I interacted with information even at just a small level. The information was closer to me. I could get access to it.

Information no longer lives only at school or in encyclopedias, and students need not depend purely on their teachers' knowledge or discretion for access to information. The Internet and web-based tools provide users with access to information 24/7. This relatively recent shift has significant ramifications for education, raising such questions as

• What factors should educators take into consideration when they encourage students to use the Internet to access information?

• How can educators help students learn to select information thoughtfully, when there is so much out there?

• Should educators encourage students to use all forms of technology (e.g., smartphones, MP3 players, notebook computers, and tablets) to access information during instructional time?

There is an important difference between having an information surplus and knowing what to do with all the information. Once teachers and administrators make the mental shift that informating is a necessity in 21st century classrooms, they need to help students build their knowledge and understanding of what it means to be informationally literate through authentic applications and meaningful performance tasks.

Amplifying

The final gradation on the enhancement-transformation continuum is *amplifying*, or broadcasting students' voices to a local or global audience. Amplifying encourages students to collaborate not only with their own classmates but also with people from around the world. Because amplifying broadens students' potential audience and pool of collaborators, students need to think critically about their tasks, purposes, and audiences. As a teacher shared during a training session we conducted, "Amplification equals locally or globally connected publishing, feedback, relearning, refining, and publishing again."

Like curriculum transformation as a whole, amplifying is not meant to be, or have, an endpoint. It is an ongoing process that benefits from collaborative input and continual upgrades. Rosenthal Tolisano (2011a) provides examples of six degrees of amplification (the higher the number, the greater the amplification):

1. Share student work with the entire class using a private collaborative tool.

2. Share your students' work with other classes in your grade level or school using a private collaborative tool.

3. Place your students' work on a classroom or school website that is not password protected.

4. Curate by organizing, tagging, and categorizing students' collective work to share online.

5. Tweet the link to your students' work to your digital learning networks (DLNs) to increase traffic to the site.

6. Connect to peers, experts, and eyewitnesses from around the world to discuss a specific topic that your students have addressed in their work and encourage feedback and exchange of ideas and perspectives.

Rosenthal Tolisano has modified these examples slightly since her original blog post and plans to continue fine-tuning them as her practice evolves and as conversations with fellow practitioners influence her thoughts and ideas. This modification process exemplifies what amplification is meant to be: living, breathing, and informed by ongoing communication and collaboration.

During the curriculum transformation process, it is important for educators to be conscious of where their upgrade lies on the *automating-informating-amplifying* continuum. We recommend giving teachers and administrators opportunities to brainstorm examples of upgrades at different points along the continuum to help shape their understanding of the different stages. For example, during a transformational workshop we conducted, a table of middle school teachers came up with the following three ways to upgrade a traditional oral report on their state's role in the U.S. Civil War:

- For an *augmentation automating* task, students could write their oral reports using a cloud-based word-processing tool, like Google Docs, that the teacher accesses to provide each student with feedback. After the teacher approves the reports, each student uses the teacher-selected web-based tool, such as ClassWiz.com, to create note cards to use when presenting the traditional oral report.

- For a *modification informating* task, a team of two or three students could use word-processing software to write a script for a one-act play geared to a specific audience or grade level and use a visual-imaging software program such as Xtranormal to create the scenery to be displayed during the live production of the play.

- For an *amplifying* task, students could create a video or multimedia presentation in a documentary format that incorporates narration, historical documents and images, and interview clips of historians discussing the state's participation in the U.S. Civil War. The students might publish the documentary on the Internet using a web-based tool such as SlideShare, YouTube, or Glogster that solicits feedback from a global audience, and they can discuss comments left by viewers (or correspond with commenters, when appropriate) to continue their learning process.

When they engage in a meaningful amplifying task, students collaborate, invite multiple perspectives, and make themselves open to learning more about a particular topic or concept. These tasks dovetail with the Common Core's English Language Arts CCR Capacities, preparing students for the world they will graduate into and interact within. The majority of students born in (and just before) the 21st century already function this way. They perceive social networking and knowledge access as ubiquitous with the use of technology and web-based tools. Lynch (2011) found that 38 percent of students "cannot go more than 10 minutes without checking in with their laptops, smartphones, tablets, or e-readers," and she noted a significant "shift from paper to digital devices for writing papers, doing research, taking class notes, and making class presentations." The current generation, and those yet to come, should not have to go back in time when they come to school (Jacobs, 2010). Teachers must ensure that their classrooms use technology and web-based tools not only for informating and amplifying but also to authentically engage students in owning their learning and producing learning opportunities for others.

TECHformational Matrices

Some schools and districts have an abundance of hardware and software as well as lightning-fast Internet access, while others have more limited resources and bandwidth. Some schools and districts have fully open Internet access and usage policies, while others have firewalls so strict that students and teachers cannot even access popular educational sites. The reality is that teachers and students need to work with what they have.

Educators preparing to transform their curriculum might want to survey their school or district's available hardware, software, and Internet access. Here is a portion of a 21st Century Pledge that one group of teachers generated during their curriculum transformation process (Jacobs, 2010):

> Each teacher commits to . . .
> - Review all current available technological resources in the district.
>   - Online resources: video streaming, Internet websites and subscriptions, WebQuest creation, webcasting through laptop.
>   - Hardware resources: videoconferencing, laptop labs, digital cameras, digital recording studio.
>   - Creative software: Movie Maker, MediaPlayer, video clips via digital cameras.
> - Identify at least one specific unit to revise.
> - Plan to replace a specific content, skill, and assessment practice with a 21st century upgrade within the unit.
> - Share the proposed change with colleagues.
> - Learn to use the tool that will be requisite to replace the current unit design with the new practice.
> - Revise the unit and begin implementation with students.
> - Tolerate a certain degree of frustration.
> - Celebrate the victories.
> - Review and share 21st century learning openly with colleagues at targeted work sessions through the school year. (p. 22)

It is important to remember that incorporating technology and web-based tools does not necessarily equal a *transform* upgrade. To visually represent the intersection of the four upgrade zones with the *automating-informating-amplifying* continuum, we developed *TECHformational matrices* on the basis of the transformational matrix (see Figure 1.2, p. 13). Each TECHformational matrix represents how using a particular technology or web-based tool in each upgrade zone influences student learning and engagement. In this chapter, we provide examples of two TECHformational matrices: one for interactive whiteboards (Figure 3.2) and one for backchanneling (Figure 3.3).

FIGURE
3.2   TECHformational Matrix: Interactive Whiteboards

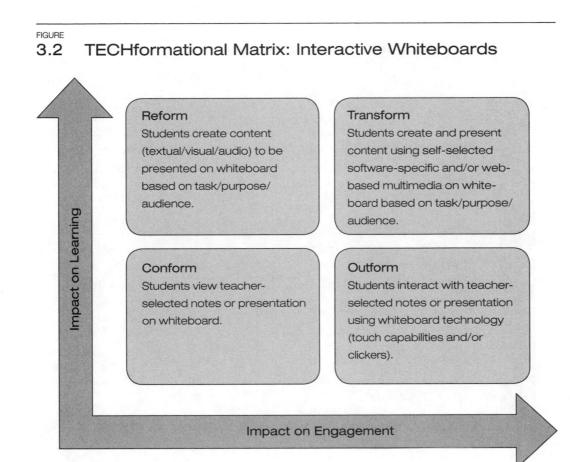

Here is how it might look to incorporate interactive whiteboards in each of the four upgrade zones:

• **Conform.** The interaction with the whiteboard is teacher-centered rather than student-centered; students' role is simply to view the teacher-created notes or presentation on the whiteboard. The assumption is that learning is taking place because students see the information. This is an example of a *substitution automating* task. The teacher has simply replaced writing on a chalkboard or holding up illustrations, photographs, or graphic organizers with using a whiteboard.

• **Outform.** Students are more engaged as they physically interact with the whiteboard using clickers, touching the screen, and writing on the screen with interactive pens. This is an example of an *augmentation automating* task; the transformation is still largely aesthetic, but students are making contributions based on what the teacher has created or selected.

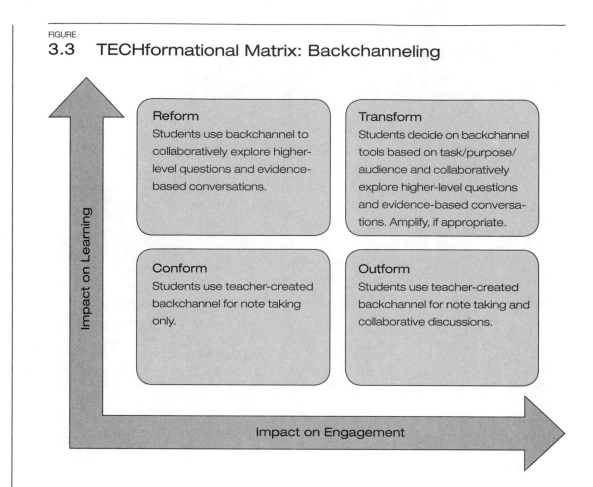

FIGURE
3.3   TECHformational Matrix: Backchanneling

- **Reform.** Students create content to be displayed on the interactive white-board rather than simply reacting to what has been created or selected by the teacher. Students must consider the *task* (what they are being asked to do); the *purpose* (why they have to do it); and the *audience* (whom are they creating the content for). Although the reform zone requires deeper thinking, this task can be accomplished without a technological tool; the interactive whiteboard is not necessary. Therefore, this is another *augmentation automating* experience for the students.

- **Transform.** This zone represents student-centered learning and engagement. Students not only create content but also choose the software and web-based tools they will use based on task, purpose, and audience. The teacher facilitates students' decision making, often by providing a rubric or other measurement tool to aid students in their thought processes. Students are authentically engaged in purposeful higher-order thinking. This is an example of a *modification* or *redefinition informating* task. Although this example does not explicitly include *amplifying*, the task can reach this stage on the continuum if students collect or curate their information online or publish their work and solicit local and global feedback.

Backchanneling is a background conversation tool similar to Twitter, with the same 140-character limit for each post. Backchanneling rooms—spaces on the Internet dedicated to a particular group or event—are private and shared via a website or designated Twitter hashtag (e.g., #ASCD2013, #cmi2013, #MitchellsonGrade5). Participants post questions or ideas on a given topic. Teachers often use the posted content to inform learning and in-the-moment teaching by addressing questions and evident misconceptions. Some students post comments as a way to share their thoughts without having to literally voice their ideas and opinions. A common practice by both teachers and students is to archive the final feed of posted comments, conversations, and questions on a given topic for later use or reference. Digital devices such as smartphones and tablets have made backchanneling viable for engaging higher-order thinking on a topic, theme, or concept.

Figure 3.3 depicts the TECHformational matrix for backchanneling.

Here is how it might look to incorporate backchanneling in each of the four upgrade zones:

- **Conform.** Students use backchanneling for personal or pseudo-collaborative note taking. Rather than creating a conversation by interacting with what the teacher (or speaker) is sharing and one another's postings, they are using the tool to take linear notes. This is an example of a *substitution automating* task: the pencil is now a keyboard, and the paper is now a digital tool.

- **Outform.** Students do online what they could not do on paper: engage in real-time conversations and access one another's thoughts without disrupting the teacher or speaker. Some students prefer to share their thoughts silently; backchanneling provides a forum for this. Because a name or call sign is associated with each post, students are recognized and honored even when they are not talking aloud. Although many students consider this form of backchanneling more motivating and engaging than trying to participate in a verbal conversation, it is not necessarily improving learning. Therefore, this might still be considered a *substitution automating* experience. If the teacher or speaker truly modified his or her instruction or presentation based on the real-time postings, this could be considered an *augmentation automating* experience.

- **Reform.** Student interactions require them to collaboratively dig deeper cognitively. Using the backchanneling room to collect their thoughts and answers to higher-order questions—singly or in groups—and prove their reasoning adds a dynamic not present in the conform and outform zones. Although these in-depth collaborative conversations demand higher-level cognitive and metacognitive skills, the process does not necessarily produce a high level of engagement. In other words, the students are doing what they are told to do using an online tool rather than responding orally or on paper. Still, this tool enables the teacher or speaker to consider what students have shared and to adapt a lesson or presentation based on the backchannel posts. Therefore, this is an example of a *modification informating* task.

- **Transform.** To shift to *redefinition informating* or *amplifying*, students need to have some control over what they are collecting within the backchannel based on task, purpose, and audience. The students are making decisions, most likely collaboratively with peers (and possibly with others, locally or globally), about the backchannel tools they will use as well as the focus of what they will collect and post.

The Appendix (p. 151) includes 12 additional TECHformational matrices that we divided into three categories: *digital devices, web-based tools,* and *curations*.

The Task, Not the Tools

During the appraising process, which we explain in Chapter 4, teachers should focus on integrating technology and web-based tools in a way that creates *transform* upgrades that *informate* or *amplify* students' learning. One caveat: anything that creates a sense of novelty when first introduced can eventually become rote. If students begin to grow weary of a particular technology, web-based tool, or upgraded unit of study, consider what needs to change to once again cognitively engage students. Consider consulting the students themselves, because they are often more familiar with the latest software applications and web-based tools and have interesting ideas about what they should be learning and about what kinds of tasks constitute authentic learning.

Keep in mind that the most important factor in upgrading a unit of study is to make the classroom a student-centered learning environment. Any technology and web-based tools integrated into a unit should fit the task. *It is the task that matters, not the tools.* Current technology and web-based tools will eventually be replaced with new ones developed by visionaries who may currently be in your classroom. It is important to build a foundation of good instruction and facilitation of learning, performance-based tasks, and purposeful technology use that enables students to apply their knowledge and skills authentically and appropriately.

In a blog post discussing *The Atlantic*'s second annual Technologies in Education forum, Busteed (2012) observes,

> A technological revolution is happening in the world of education; it is changing schools for the better. But, it will never change the definition of and need for great teaching. . . . You would think that a room full of "who's who" technology experts, online and gaming companies, and futurists would "talk tech." We had that conversation to be sure. But the intriguing part was that the discussion kept returning to the basics of great classroom teaching. There was widespread agreement among the participants that technology will change everything *and* nothing. Essentially, what we do with technology has to have fundamental underpinnings in what the best teachers in the world have done for decades. (paras. 1–2)

John F. Kennedy and Busteed are in agreement: *educators are extraordinary*. As teachers collaborate to transform curriculum, their students will be encouraged and empowered to think creatively and lead effectively for decades to come.

Discussion Questions

1. Consider the differences among the points on the *automating-informating-amplifying* continuum. What questions or concerns arise about your current learning and teaching practices? What recurring issues, based on possible misconceptions about the integration of technology and web-based tools, might be affecting your school or district?

2. The explanations of the two TECHformational matrices in this chapter draw a connection between the upgrade zones of the transformational matrix and the *automating-informating-amplifying* continuum. What thoughts come to mind as you process the descriptions provided for the four matrix zones in the two bulleted lists (pp. 35–38)? How might these descriptions influence your own upcoming upgrades?

3. Take a few minutes to study the 12 TECHformational matrices included in the Appendix (p. 151). Pick one matrix from each category (digital devices, web-based tools, and curations) and discuss the learning and teaching implications for each matrix with your colleagues. The Appendix's introduction (p. 152) includes a few questions you might use to spark conversations.

4

The Transformation Spiral

The human mind always makes progress, but it is a progress in spirals.

—Madame de Stael

The term *cycle* is often used to explain a sequence of events taking place over time; in education, the term often refers to changes and professional growth in instructional practice and curriculum design. But Costa and Kallick (1995) explain why this growth is better described as a *spiral* than a loop (or cycle):

> We were pleased with the [feedback loop] concept until we decided loops imply that a learner is in the same state or condition at the "end" of a circle as at the beginning. Loops suggest returning to the same place. Spirals, however, imply a recursive process. They are not intended to define bottom line, summative, or terminal conditions or behaviors. . . . As Heroclitus observes, "You can never step into the river of time twice." When a person steps into a river, neither the river nor the person will be the same again. They have both changed from the experience. A feedback spiral reflects this experience where a feedback loop does not. (pp. 25–26)

Teachers who aim to transform their curriculum do not want to go backward or stay in the same place after the upgraded unit of study has ended; rather, they want to upgrade the same unit of study again, or upgrade a new unit of study.

To begin the transformation spiral, teachers must focus on upgrading specific elements of the existing curriculum thoughtfully and gradually (Jacobs, 2010). The transformational process consists of four phases:

- Appraisal and brainstorming.
- Commitment and communication.
- Reactions and reflections.
- Revisions.

Each phase enables teachers to upgrade units of study in purposeful ways. Together, the phases present a natural sequence for making conscientious decisions and reflecting on the results of those decisions. In the following sections, we describe the processes of each of these phases and show how they fit into the transformation spiral.

Appraising and Brainstorming

During the appraisal and brainstorming phase, teachers determine which unit of study they will upgrade. Curriculum transformation is best accomplished gradually, so, although multiple units may be worthy of upgrade, teachers will need to agree on one unit or series of lesson plans.

Determining which transformational lens or lenses (see Chapter 2) teachers will incorporate into the upgrade is the first process in this phase. Although there is no right or wrong lens to apply to a particular unit of study, some units will naturally lend themselves to certain lenses. The questions to pose when appraising units of study may vary depending on the teachers, curriculum, and administrative requisites involved. Here are a few questions to consider when evaluating potential units to upgrade:

- Which transformational lenses are the most important to integrate into the upgraded unit of study?
- Which specific content standards and CCSS for English Language Arts CCR Capacities or Standards for Mathematical Practice need to be considered?
- Which units of study would be conducive to upgrades based on integration of technology and web-based tools?
- Which units of study have the most potential for encouraging students to own their own learning?
- Are there any directives based on school or district action plans that might influence which units should be considered for upgrading?

Once teachers have narrowed down the potential units to upgrade to one, or possibly two, it is time to brainstorm answers to these three questions:

• Whose orbits of ability will be needed to aid in a successful upgrade?

• What specific technology or web-based tools will the upgrade require to promote *informating* and *amplifying?*

• Will the upgrade affect the length of the unit of study? If so, how would this change affect other units of study that must be addressed during the school year?

As we have emphasized throughout Part 1, transforming curriculum is a collaborative effort. We recommend creating digital learning networks (DLNs) to establish local and global connections. Networking could aid teachers in locating an orbit of ability that is needed to upgrade a particular unit of study. People whose orbits of ability are critical to a unit's upgrade do not need to contribute in person; they may play a role virtually, through videoconferencing, phone calls, or e-mails. Once a transformation team is formed, it is important to establish a sense of trust and openness because team members need to feel safe and able to ask questions as they go through their own personal growth processes.

Technology and web-based tools play a crucial role in both *outform* and *transform* curriculum upgrades. During the brainstorming process, it is important to consider authentic technology applications that provide students with opportunities to *informate* and *amplify*.

An upgrade may or may not change the length of a unit of study. The number of transformational lenses incorporated into a unit's upgrade typically correlates with the unit's duration from implementation to conclusion. For example, when a transformation team incorporates creative and critical thinking (which falls under the lens of 21st century clarifications) and a performance task assessment (which falls under the lens of entry points) in an upgraded unit, the original unit needs to be extended to give students adequate time to process what they are learning and to authentically apply the unit's concepts, content, and skills to the performance task. Teachers we have worked with find that adding time to a unit is worthwhile because it enables students to better transfer and generalize what they have learned.

Commitment and Communication

The definition of *commitment* that best defines a transformational mind-set is "the state of being bound emotionally or intellectually to a course of action" (The Free

Dictionary, n.d.). At the beginning of the commitment and communication phase, those involved in planning and implementing the upgraded unit need to recognize the level of commitment that the transformation requires. Depending on the complexity of the upgrade, the commitment may involve steep learning curves with regard to standards, content, skills, assessments, or the use of technology or web-based tools.

The term *communication* refers to the exchanges that take place both before and during implementation of the unit of study. The transformation team may meet daily, weekly, or as needed during preparation and implementation. As teachers prepare for a unit, they have a lot to consider, including the acquisition of necessary resources and materials and the planning of activities, formative assessments, the performance task assessment, and the culminating experience, if there is one. Because this phase of the process includes what takes place before as well as during the implementation of an upgraded unit, the Commitment and Communication section of each transformational snapshot in Part 2 is the most detailed.

Reactions and Reflections

After we watch a movie or attend a special event, discussing our reactions and reflecting on what took place is a natural process. Quite often, when teachers implement an upgraded unit of study, they have reactions and reflections while the unit is taking place. Some teachers prefer to write down anecdotes during the unit, while others prefer to talk through what has been or is currently happening. Whatever teachers prefer to do during the unit, we recommend that at the conclusion of the unit, the transformation team archive its reactions and reflections as soon as possible using a desired written format, such as hard-copy journal entries, word-processing documents saved to a hard drive or network, or an online writing tool such as Google Docs. It is important to capture *in print* what worked well and what did not work as well. It is also important to record ideas for modification for future use of the unit of study or for reference in transforming another unit of study. Although there are no specific mandatory questions to ask during this phase, here are a few questions that teams typically address:

• Were the transformational lenses evident as planned in the upgraded unit of study?

• What instructional modifications were made *in the moment* to ensure that the desired transformation took place?

- What instructional modifications were made to ensure that all learners were successful?
- What instructional modifications are being considered for the next implementation of the upgraded unit of study?
- What were students' reactions at the beginning, during, and at the end of the upgraded unit of study?

Transformation team members may also want to include students' comments and suggestions as a way to jog their memories when they look back at their own reactions and reflections during the next academic year.

Revisions

Revisions refer to the additions or changes made to an upgraded unit of study after a significant time has passed since the completion of the upgraded unit. Ideas for revision can come from many sources, including purposeful ongoing investigation, conversations with colleagues, a chance find online, connections made through established or new DLNs, or a professional resource, such as a journal. These influences result in a transformation team's continued commitment to improve a particular unit of study.

The Spiral in Action

The transformational snapshots in Part 2 illustrate what these four phases look like in action. Because no two classrooms or experiences are exactly alike, each snapshot tells its own story, and each story has its own spiral element based on teachers' reflections and revisions. When spiraling, or further transforming, an upgraded unit of study, you might consider modifying existing lenses or adding a new one. For example, a transformation team may choose to revisit the CCSS for English Language Arts CCR Capacities to explore how to better combine one or two capacities with the unit's content.

Discussion Questions

1. Which of the transformational process's four phases (appraisal and brainstorming, commitment and communication, reactions and reflections, revisions) do you find the most intriguing, and why?

2. As Costa and Kallick (1995) point out, there is a difference between a *cycle* and a *spiral*. When you read the first section of this chapter, what came to mind as you conceptualized a *cyclical* curriculum design process versus a *spiral* curriculum design process?

3. How has the explanation of each upgrade zone in Chapter 1, along with the information provided in Chapters 2 through 4, shaped your understanding of what the four upgrade zones involve for students and teachers?

Part II

Transformational
Snapshots

In an episode of *Who Do You Think You Are?* featuring actress Rita Wilson, the producers displayed a snapshot of Rita with her father, Allan, as an elderly gentleman. The next snapshot depicted Allan as a young immigrant who had just come to the United States from Bulgaria. It struck us that although both photos showed the same person, transformations had taken place between the times the photos were taken. Each snapshot was a story capturing a moment in time. Richard Bach (n.d.), author of *Jonathan Livingston Seagull*, observed, "Snapshots don't show the million decisions that led to that moment," and we agree. We hope that Part 2 of this book captures the essence of the critical decisions that the educators profiled made as they transformed learning and teaching.

What the Snapshots Look Like

We wanted to begin this section with a transformational lesson plan ("Ten-Frame Mathematics") to convey that upgrading learning and teaching does not always require modifying an entire unit of study. The remaining eight snapshots represent upgraded units of study. At the onset of each snapshot, a table lists the specific transformational lenses that the lesson or unit includes, from the following four categories:

- *Entry points,* as described in Chapter 2, include performance task assessments, culminating experiences, curriculum examinations, and instructional innovations.
- *21st century clarifications* include higher-order thinking, collaborative environments, local and global connections, and glocal impacts.
- *Technology authenticity,* as addressed in Chapter 3, includes technology tools and web-based tools.
- *Standards connections* for the Common Core State Standards for English Language Arts CCR Capacities or Standards for Mathematical Practice are included if relevant to a snapshot's discipline or focus.

Each table also specifies whether the snapshot fits in the *outform* or the *transform* upgrade zone. We chose to highlight these two zones because of the greater emphasis they place on the use of technology and web-based tools.

After the transformational lenses table, each chapter follows the transformation team through the four phases of the transformational process: appraisal and brainstorming, commitment and communication, reactions and reflections, and revisions.

At the end of each snapshot, we include discussion questions. Please join us online at ASCD EDge to collaboratively discuss these questions and much more in our Curriculum Transformations group (edge.ascd.org).

5

Ten-Frame Mathematics

Transformational Lenses		
Entry Points	**21st Century Clarifications**	**Technology Authenticity**
• Instructional innovations	• Higher-order thinking • Collaborative environments	• Technology tools
Standards Connections		

Standards for Mathematical Practice

• Make sense of problems and persevere in solving them.

• Reason abstractly and quantitatively.

• Model with mathematics.

• Use appropriate tools strategically.

Transformational Matrix Upgrade Zone: Transform

Mrs. Stevenson's state recently embraced the Common Core State Standards, and her district has set expectations for creating a 21st century learning environment. Mrs. Stevenson, who has taught kindergarten for almost 20 years, has been attending various trainings provided by the state and district both virtually and in person—such as a series of state-sponsored webinars for kindergarten teachers explaining critical changes in mathematical learning expectations. For example, patterning concepts are being taught in new ways: the standards no longer focus on having students determine a core pattern (e.g., ABB), extend the core pattern two or three times, and then create their own core and extended patterns. Instead, the Common Core State Standards for Mathematics for kindergarten emphasize developing foundational concepts of the base-ten number system.

Appraisal and Brainstorming

In the late spring, Mrs. Stevenson attended a districtwide workshop on upgrading curriculum and instruction for kindergarten and 1st grade. Throughout the morning, the facilitators discussed ways to increase students' ownership of their learning and authentically integrate technology and web-based tools into instruction. After lunch, the teachers split into small groups to begin thinking about upgrading a lesson or series of lessons based on either the Common Core State Standards for Mathematics (CCSSM) or the Common Core State Standards for English Language Arts and Literacy (CCSS for ELA) and the integration of technology or web-based tools.

The teachers at Mrs. Stevenson's table discussed the Common Core options and decided to divide into two groups, with one group focusing on upgrading a CCSSM-based lesson and the other focusing on upgrading a CCSS for ELA–based lesson. Mrs. Stevenson chose to work with two colleagues—Mrs. Brumpton, a fellow kindergarten teacher from her school, and Mr. Lee, a 1st grade teacher from another school—on a CCSSM-based kindergarten lesson. Because the current school year was the first year of CCSSM implementation in the district, many teachers were still trying to make sense of the Standards for Mathematical Practice as well as the new content. They knew their lesson plan would need to combine mathematical practices with content standards. They also discussed the requirement for authentically integrating technology or web-based tools.

5.1   Decomposition Example

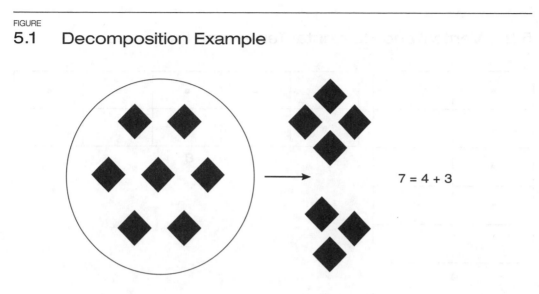

$$7 = 4 + 3$$

After reviewing the content that was being learned at this time of the year, the group decided to focus on *subitizing*, or the process of accurately and fluently judging number quantities regardless of array (scattered placement of objects). During this period of the school year, the kindergartners were working on decomposing sets of up to 10 objects (see Figure 5.1) as well as using ten-frames, a visual tool that aids in counting and builds students' understanding of number relationships (see Figure 5.2).

Commitment and Communication

Mrs. Stevenson shared that she could envision either a decomposition lesson or a ten-frame lesson, during which students would work with manipulatives while she displayed sets (for the decomposition lesson) or ten-frame images (for the ten-frame lesson) on the interactive whiteboard. Mr. Lee asked her to describe a typical lesson for each concept. After listening to her description, he suggested combining the two concepts so that students would use a ten-frame as a visual aid while using critical thinking to figure out possible combinations of decomposed sets of 5 or 10. Mrs. Stevenson and Mrs. Brumpton asked him to explain his idea in further detail.

Mr. Lee explained that his school's predominant focus this year had been on the Common Core's Standards for Mathematical Practice—specifically, "Make sense of

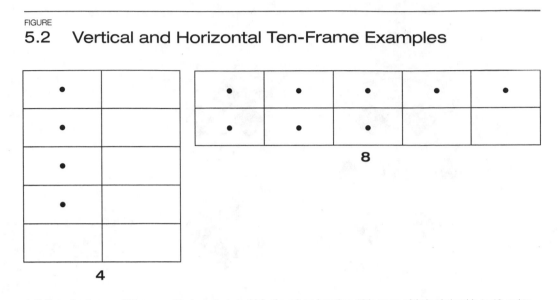

5.2　Vertical and Horizontal Ten-Frame Examples

Activities using frames of 10 squares teach students to think of numbers less than 10 in terms of their relationship to 10 and to build a sound knowledge of the basic addition and subtraction facts for 10, which are an integral part of mental calculation.

problems and persevere in solving them" and "Model with mathematics." He said that at the beginning of the year, he often had to remind himself that *modeling* does not mean *using manipulatives*; rather, it means having students learn by using real-life, authentic situations. He and his colleagues found that having students solve higher-order thinking tasks had improved their cognitive processing, and he had recently read a book that emphasized higher-order thinking in mathematics lessons for 1st graders. He was picturing one lesson in particular that he thought could be adapted for kindergarten learning.

The lesson would begin with the teacher saying, "The pet store in our local mall has 10 pets for sale. What is the number of different pets for sale?" Mrs. Brumpton thought for a moment and responded, "It could be anything: dogs, cats, fish, turtles . . . even iguanas!" Mr. Lee said that was the point: getting students to think about what is known and what is unknown and to ask clarifying questions. For example, he would want students to ask him, "What kinds of pets does the store sell?" Mrs. Stevenson was intrigued but thought the lesson presented too difficult a cognitive task for kindergartners. She suggested providing more detail in the problem: "The pet store in our local mall has *5* pets for sale. What is the number of different pets for sale if the store sells *cats* and *birds?*" Mrs. Brumpton agreed that this phrasing was more appropriate for kindergartners.

Mr. Lee then briefly explained what he envisioned for the remaining steps of the lesson. Mrs. Stevenson and Mrs. Brumpton loved his idea. They believed the lesson would both challenge their students to be higher-order thinkers and incorporate CCSSM-based patterning expectations.

At this point, one of the facilitators, Mr. Gilbert, came over to the teachers' table and asked about their appraisal and brainstorming. After they shared their ideas, he agreed that what they had planned would be an excellent lesson in terms of both upgrading the curriculum and incorporating the Standards for Mathematical Practice. He then questioned Mrs. Stevenson further:

Mr. Gilbert: How do you picture yourself using the interactive whiteboard during the lesson?

Mrs. Stevenson: As I share the problem with my students, I would show a photograph of the mall and then a photograph of the pet store. At the appropriate time, I would display ten-frames on the screen and use them to represent the possible combinations of cats and birds while my students use cardstock ten-frames and counter chips. Finally, I would display photographs of cats and birds as I reveal clues for each possible pet.

Mr. Gilbert: How is this lesson interactive?

Mrs. Stevenson: To me, *interactive* means *engaging*. My students enjoy my use of the interactive whiteboard. For example, I once used the whiteboard to show my students time-lapse videos of various types of plants growing from seed to adult. The students were mesmerized as they observed the plants' growing stages, and afterward they participated in a meaningful discussion of what they had observed.

Mr. Gilbert: How was students' observation of the plants' growth interactive?

Mrs. Stevenson: My students were cognitively stimulated as they observed actual plants growing in rapid sequence rather than looking at static pictures in a book.

Mr. Gilbert: But there was no literal interaction with the whiteboard. For example, you could have had students mark parts of the plant using the whiteboard's interactive pens. I'll illustrate my point. What is your favorite television show?

Mrs. Stevenson: I enjoy watching *Dancing with the Stars*.

Mr. Gilbert: Is watching the show an *interactive* or a *reactive* experience?

Mrs. Stevenson: [Thinks for a moment.] At first, I was going to say it's an *interactive* experience because I feel as if I am literally dancing with the stars. I get caught up in their emotions, and I am able to vote by phone for my favorite team at the end of each episode. But now, based on our discussion, I'm thinking it is a *reactive* experience.

Mr. Gilbert: Right. When you and Mrs. Brumpton teach the upgraded lesson, you need to make sure that students interact tactilely with the whiteboard rather than merely react to content you provide.

Soon it was time to conclude the workshop. Mrs. Stevenson and Mrs. Brumpton thanked Mr. Lee for his help in creating their kindergarten lesson and told him that they would teach the lesson in the next week or two and e-mail him to let him know how it went.

On the day of the lesson, Mrs. Stevenson divided her students into teams of three, which she purposefully arranged to create a balance of mathematical and language capabilities, and had them sit on the rug in front of the interactive whiteboard. She gave each group a ten-frame grid, five counter chips that were red on one side and yellow on the other, a small dry-erase board, and a dry-erase marker.

Mrs. Stevenson began the lesson by displaying a photograph of the local mall on the interactive whiteboard and asking if anyone enjoyed going to the mall. After listening to students' responses, she displayed a photograph of the pet storefront inside the mall. The students erupted in conversation about the pet store and their own pets. Mrs. Stevenson told them that she and her husband had been walking in the mall recently and saw a sign in the pet store window that read "Pets for Sale." She and Mr. Stevenson walked inside and asked how many pets were for sale. The store clerk said that he had five pets for sale, some of which were cats and some birds.

Mrs. Stevenson then shared the task question with the class: "How many of each kind of pet—cats and birds—were for sale that day?" She asked the teams to brainstorm possible combinations of cats and birds that might have been for sale. She knew that some students would have difficulty, given the level of thinking the task required, so she walked among the teams as they brainstormed and aided students who were struggling.

After a few minutes, Mrs. Stevenson asked the teams to share the combinations they had come up with. One team shared two combinations: no cats and five birds, and five cats and no birds. Before Mrs. Stevenson could respond, a student from another team exclaimed, "That can't happen. The store clerk said there were *some* cats and *some* birds, so there has to be at least one cat and one bird."

Mrs. Stevenson acknowledged that it is sometimes difficult to talk about sets or quantities without seeing them and noted that some students had chosen to use the manipulatives they had been given as they discussed the problem. Mrs. Stevenson asked Marissa, who had been manipulating the chips during the brainstorming session, to share what she was thinking. Marissa shared that she had used both sides of the chips to help her come up with combinations: red to represent cats and yellow to represent birds. A student sitting nearby exclaimed that that was a good idea. The students started to chatter within their teams and began creating sets that included various combinations of chip colors. Mrs. Stevenson noticed that some teams laid the chips directly on the dry-erase boards, while others represented their combinations using the ten-frames.

While the students focused on creating various two-color combinations, Mrs. Stevenson used the interactive whiteboard to display a T-chart whose two columns were labeled *Cats* and *Birds*. After waiting a few more moments, she asked the students to look at the whiteboard. She mentioned that she had heard them describing different combinations of pets and wanted to record the possible combinations on the T-chart using numbers. She asked different students to come in turn to the whiteboard and use an interactive pen to record the numbers representing each possible combination on the T-chart. Then Mrs. Stevenson said she would like to rewrite the combinations in a particular order because she noticed something interesting. After reordering the combinations, she asked the students if they noticed a pattern (see Figure 5.3).

Almost all of the students said they saw the numbers going higher on the left side and lower on the right side. Mrs. Stevenson then used the interactive whiteboard to display four blank ten-frames, red dots, and yellow dots. She suggested that the students use their own ten-frames and colored chips to represent each combination and then write each combination as an equation on their dry-erase boards. She asked Miguel to come up and help her represent the first combination recorded on the T-chart: one cat and four birds. He touched the screen with his finger to move one red dot into the left column of the ten-frame and four yellow dots into the right column. Mrs. Stevenson then guided him as he wrote the decomposition equation

5.3   Cats and Birds T-Chart

Cats	Birds
1	4
2	3
3	2
4	1

for the ten-frame representation: $5 = 1 + 4$. The rest of the students used manipulatives to display the same combination on their own ten-frames and wrote the equation on their dry-erase boards.

Next, Mrs. Stevenson asked each team to represent the next combination—two cats and three birds—on their ten-frames and write the equation for that combination. After providing adequate time, Mrs. Stevenson asked a different student to come to the interactive whiteboard to display the combination on another blank ten-frame and write the decomposition equation. She repeated this process until all of the possible combinations and equations were displayed on the whiteboard (see Figure 5.4).

After the class studied the displayed pictorial (ten-frames) and abstract (equations) results, Mrs. Stevenson said, "It's time to figure out which combination represents the actual number of cats and birds that were for sale at the pet store." She added a new window to the interactive screen that displayed five large question marks and asked a student to come up and touch one of the question marks. When the student touched the screen, the question mark dissolved to reveal a photograph of a cockatiel. The students began to talk among themselves. One student excitedly called out that the combination must be $5 = 4 + 1$ because the first pet revealed was a bird. Mrs. Stevenson said, "You'll have to put your thinking caps on tightly because there are still four more question marks to reveal, and there may be more birds." She reminded the students that all four possible combinations included at least one bird and pointed to the dots in each ten-frame's *Birds* column.

FIGURE

5.4   Possible Ten-Frame Pet Combinations

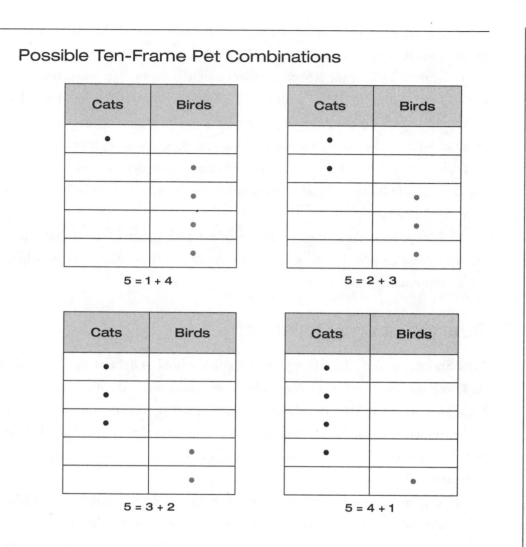

Cats	Birds
●	
	●
	●
	●
	●

5 = 1 + 4

Cats	Birds
●	
●	
	●
	●
	●

5 = 2 + 3

Cats	Birds
●	
●	
●	
	●
	●

5 = 3 + 2

Cats	Birds
●	
●	
●	
●	
	●

5 = 4 + 1

When the next student called on touched the screen, a Persian cat appeared. With Mrs. Stevenson's facilitation, the class agreed that all four combinations were still possible because each ten-frame included at least one cat and one bird.

The next pet revealed was a parrot. The students immediately reviewed what they knew: there were at least two birds and one cat for sale. Mrs. Stevenson asked, "Which of the ten-frames and equations no longer work as a representation of the number of cats and birds for sale at the pet store?" Through discussion, facilitation, and collaborative decision making, the students decided they could eliminate the ten-frame and equation representing 5 = 4 + 1 because it represented only one bird. Mrs. Stevenson asked a student to come to the whiteboard to draw an X through this ten-frame and equation with an interactive pen.

The fourth pet revealed was a calico kitten. After further discussion, the students decided to eliminate the ten-frame and equation representing $5 = 1 + 4$.

Charlotte came to the whiteboard and touched the final question mark, revealing a canary. Some of the students could barely contain their excitement. Mrs. Stevenson explained the thinking process for students who were not as quick to realize that the logical solution was the ten-frame and equation representing two cats and three birds ($5 = 2 + 3$). She then facilitated a discussion on what would have happened had Charlotte touched the question mark and revealed a long-haired cat instead of a canary.

Mrs. Stevenson concluded the lesson by reminding her students that it is important to always look for patterns and think about how those patterns can help us solve mathematical problems.

Reactions and Reflections

Mrs. Stevenson and Mrs. Brumpton met after school to debrief the lesson that they had both used in their classrooms. They were quite pleased with the results. Mrs. Stevenson thanked Mrs. Brumpton for helping her upload the photographs and make the ten-frames, dot images, and question marks that she had needed for the lesson, since she was not yet comfortable operating the interactive whiteboard's software tools.

Mrs. Brumpton commented, "I definitely think that the Standards for Mathematical Practice we identified were seen and heard when I taught the lesson." Mrs. Stevenson agreed and added, "My students also exhibited the practice 'Construct viable arguments and critique the reasoning of others' when they proposed and discussed ideas for possible combinations of pets." After some more discussion about how the lesson played out in both classrooms, they finalized their thoughts in a Microsoft Word document that they saved on the network drive in a folder titled "Transformation Reflections":

• **Critical thinking:** Students had to think critically to figure out the possible combinations for the pet store task as well as use a process of logical elimination to reach a final combination. They also used critical thinking to determine if their final selection was accurate.

• **Collaboration and communication:** While working in teams and as a whole group, the students truly worked together to solve the task. Both classes' students waited patiently for classmates who were struggling with the higher-order thinking necessary to solve the task (e.g., trying to figure out if a particular combination was still valid based on the pets revealed thus far). When they were not in agreement (critique), they were kind and respectful to one another.

- **Technology tools:** Using the whiteboard in a truly interactive way made the lesson more engaging for the students.

Mrs. Stevenson said she would send an e-mail to Mr. Lee to let him know how the lesson went. As she headed back to her room, Mrs. Brumpton mentioned that she now wanted to try upgrading an entire unit of study and asked if Mrs. Stevenson would like to work on the transformation process together. After Mrs. Stevenson said that she would, they agreed on a time to meet to appraise upcoming science and social studies units and select one unit to upgrade. They planned to mark the completion of the selected unit's learning through a performance task assessment or a culminating experience.

Revisions

At the end of the school year, the third kindergarten teacher in Mrs. Stevenson's school moved to another state. Over the summer, Mrs. Stevenson and Mrs. Brumpton participated in the selection process for hiring a new kindergarten teacher. They asked the candidates a variety of questions about their willingness to work collaboratively, embrace the district's curriculum expectations, and create a 21st century learning environment. After interviewing 10 prospective teachers, the school hired Ms. Swanson, a second-year teacher.

Mrs. Stevenson and Mrs. Brumpton met with Ms. Swanson approximately three weeks before teachers in the district officially returned to school. Among much that the group discussed, Mrs. Stevenson and Mrs. Brumpton shared their desire to continue to upgrade lesson plans and units of study and explained the transformation process and TECHformational matrices that they had learned about at the workshop they had attended in the spring. Ms. Swanson was excited about the process and showed them some of the web-based tools and applications she had downloaded to her tablet that might be useful in the coming year. The discussion continued:

> **Mrs. Brumpton:** We're happy that your orbit of ability is overlapping with ours!

Ms. Swanson: [Scrunches forehead.] I'm not familiar with that phrase.

Mrs. Stevenson: Every teacher has a specific ability or set of abilities that can enable and empower those around him or her to improve their own professional capabilities.

Mrs. Brumpton: Your ease in navigating the Internet to find websites and applications that could aid student learning will be an asset for us.

Ms. Swanson: I'm glad to hear that I can be helpful in this way. And since I'm still learning so much about the art of teaching, I will constantly be traveling in your orbits of ability throughout the school year!

Discussion Questions

1. This lesson represents a *transform* upgrade appropriate for a kindergarten classroom. What evidence from the snapshot shows the lesson's impact on students' learning of both mathematical content and the Standards for Mathematical Practice? What evidence shows the lesson's positive impact on engaging students through technology?

2. Mrs. Stevenson discovered that higher-order thinking provided an opportunity for students to "construct viable arguments and critique the reasoning of others." How might you upgrade a current lesson plan or unit of study to include students' authentic critiques of one another's reasoning?

3. Mrs. Stevenson and Mrs. Brumpton viewed Ms. Swanson as an asset to their kindergarten team. What orbits of ability would you appreciate your colleagues having as you work collaboratively to transform curriculum?

6

Flat Stanley Podcast

Transformational Lenses		
Entry Points	**21st Century Clarifications**	**Technology Authenticity**
• Culminating experiences • Instructional innovations	• Higher-order thinking • Collaborative environments • Global connections	• Technology tools • Web-based tools
Standards Connections		
English Language Arts College and Career Readiness Capacities • Students respond to the varying demands of audience, task, purpose, and discipline. • Students use technology and digital media strategically and capably. • Students come to understand other perspectives and cultures.		
Transformational Matrix Upgrade Zone: Transform		

Flat Stanley (Brown, 1964), a children's chapter book published almost 50 years ago, has reached classic status in many classrooms. In the book, Stanley, a young boy, is literally flattened by a falling bulletin board. He makes the best of his two-dimensional state; one particular advantage is that he can travel around the world by being mailed in an envelope.

Primary-level teachers often use this story in an integrated social studies unit that combines writing friendly correspondence with learning about different places around the world. Traditionally, each student makes a Flat Stanley paper doll and mails it to a friend or family member who, in turn, mails Stanley to a new destination. Throughout the process, letters are sent back to the class providing information about the towns Stanley has visited, plus photos of his adventures in each location. All the Flat Stanleys are mailed back to the classroom by a predetermined return date and are welcomed with a celebratory homecoming.

Mrs. Cohen, a 1st grade teacher, attended a workshop on curriculum transformation that encouraged participants to upgrade one unit of study per marking period. When asked to consider possible transformational lenses, Mrs. Cohen decided to focus on global connections, which her unit titled The World Around Us addresses with the help of Flat Stanley. She knew her challenge would be the authentic use of web-based tools and technology.

Appraisal and Brainstorming

After appraising her current units of study at the workshop and settling on The World Around Us, Mrs. Cohen observed,

> During The World Around Us, my students enjoy sending their paper Flat Stanleys to relatives and friends. I am thinking I could transform this unit to incorporate authentic global connections using technology and web-based opportunities at my school. Realistically, though, I will need help with the latter, especially the web-based world. When I get back to school, I am going to talk to one of my 1st grade colleagues, Ms. Taylor, who is quite knowledgeable when it comes to technology and web-based tools.

Once she returned to school, Mrs. Cohen shared her initial thoughts for upgrading The World Around Us with Ms. Taylor. After brainstorming potential technology and web-based tools they could integrate into the unit, they decided to upgrade the unit's culminating experience from writing and illustrating a big book to creating a podcast. They discussed how this experience would enable them to include authentic global interactions and technology software. Mrs. Cohen noted that creating a podcast would help students embrace the competency of writing for varied purposes and tasks. She observed that she would need to modify some of her instructional approaches when teaching the unit and asked Ms. Taylor if she would assist when necessary. They discovered that their specials on certain days were at different times, so that Ms. Taylor would be able to visit Mrs. Cohen's room without disrupting instructional time. Mrs. Cohen recorded the planned transformational details online in her Projected/Diary Map's unit-planning feature within the district's curriculum mapping system.

Commitment and Communication

When the time came to begin the unit, Mrs. Cohen explained to her students that she was going to learn alongside them and that Ms. Taylor would be coming in occasionally to help everyone learn. The children reacted with excitement to the idea that their teacher was going to be a fellow learner. Mrs. Cohen shared an overview of the unit and began reading *Flat Stanley* aloud. She read the story's chapters over several days.

After finishing the story and discussing its main points, Mrs. Cohen facilitated a brainstorming session in which students came up with ideas for a collaboratively written story that would likewise flatten them and send them on a traveling adventure. The students decided that their interactive whiteboard could fall off the wall to make them "as thin as a DVD!" as one student exclaimed.

Mrs. Cohen explained that students would not be making their story into a paperbound big book, their traditional method for creating class books. Instead, they would be creating a podcast. She explained that unlike a book, a podcast is not read but listened to. She then played a podcast of a familiar fairy tale using the interactive whiteboard and asked her students to think about the similarities and differences between being a *listener* and a *reader*. One student observed that listeners "have to listen carefully to hear the describing words because there are no pictures." After the follow-up discussion, Mrs. Cohen reminded her class that its story's text would need to be well written so that the words would become illustrations in the listeners' minds. The students excitedly talked among themselves about this new way to tell a story.

The unit's content focused on the Earth's land and ocean areas. To connect this learning to students' upcoming writing experience, Mrs. Cohen took the class on a visual tour of the world's continents, countries, and cities using both hands-on and virtual globes and announced that each student's Flat Self needed to visit a specific city, state, or country in the world.

Each student selected a travel destination to research, with the goal of including the destination's highlights in the podcast. Through a combination of in-class and at-home investigations with support from both the teacher and parents or guardians, each student researched his or her destination by reading and listening to informational books, looking at photographs, and using the Internet to learn about one cultural tradition, one tourist attraction, and weather patterns throughout the year.

While the students individually conducted research, they collaboratively wrote their story's introduction and conclusion with the help of Mrs. Cohen. She reminded them that they would be writing individual short descriptions about their chosen destinations that would become the middle of their podcast story.

Throughout the unit, Ms. Taylor and Mrs. Cohen continued to communicate and plan. Ms. Taylor worked with the students on storytelling techniques using a few websites and interactive digital activities, including Into the Book (www.intothe book.net). For her part, Mrs. Cohen taught students how to use expressive words to enhance the audience's listening experience by reading aloud theater scripts and having students discuss the author's purpose when using a script format.

Each student prepared a draft of his or her journey script that included the required research information:

- Where did you go? (city, state, or country)
- What were your favorite things to see and do while you were there? (cultural tradition, tourist attraction)
- What was the weather like when you were there? (based on class-determined season)

During the script-writing process, Mrs. Cohen continually reminded students that because a podcast is an audio recording, they needed to use strong descriptive words. Students worked collaboratively to revise their personal scripts' word choice, answering the following questions:

- How did it emotionally *feel* to arrive at your destination?
- How did it *sound* or *smell* at your destination?
- What did you *see* at your destination?
- What did you *touch* or *taste* at your destination?

After the students made final revisions to the story's beginning and ending and to their own journey scripts, the day finally arrived to begin recording their story. The students were excited, and giggles could be heard throughout the room. Mrs. Cohen observed the class while Ms. Taylor began recording students using Garage-Band, an audio-recording software application designed by Apple. She visually projected the recording program onto the interactive whiteboard so that everyone could experience the audio-track creation of the students' captured voices. Everyone collaboratively engaged in the process of arranging the students' personal journey segments into one coherent, fluent story. The final podcast described a variety of destinations, including the cities of London, Tokyo, New York, and Hollywood; the U.S. states of Alabama, Illinois, and Michigan; the countries of Israel and Peru; and two unique destinations, the North Pole and the Amazon River.

To continue the upgrade of the unit's culminating experience and ensure an authentic global connection, Ms. Taylor helped Mrs. Cohen upload the podcast as a link on Mrs. Cohen's newly created classroom website. Mrs. Cohen observed how Ms. Taylor created a blog post on her own website and embedded the podcast link. In the post, Ms. Taylor asked those who listened to the podcast to write a comment in the post's comment box, including their first and last names and locations. She requested that commenters who came from a location discussed by a student let the student know if his or her information was accurate and share something new that all the students could learn about the destination.

The class watched as Ms. Taylor next sent out a tweet about *Our Flat Selves* and included a link to the podcast. As she did in the blog post, she asked followers to listen to the podcast and leave a comment.

Within 24 hours, comments to Ms. Taylor's blog post started pouring in from around the world. Mrs. Cohen read aloud each comment to her students. They beamed with pride as their audience grew each day, and they were especially excited when commenters left messages directed to them by name. Ms. Taylor had added a feature to Mrs. Cohen's website that marked the location of each listener-commenter on a Google Map to visually represent how far the students' voices had traveled. They were amazed to see that their podcast had been heard around the world!

Reactions and Reflections

After the unit was completed, Mrs. Cohen and Ms. Taylor reflected on the events and lessons learned. They agreed that the upgraded culminating experience had been a success. Mrs. Cohen noted that although her main goal had been to create a web-based, globally interactive culminating experience, she was surprised at the extent to which it had also affected her instructional plans throughout the unit. She observed that even though she had faced a steep digital learning curve, the efforts paid off in heightened student engagement. Her students had become more aware and active as writers after learning that their story would have to be more engaging for listeners.

Ms. Taylor observed that although the transformation had focused on integrating technology and web-based tools, the learning expectations emphasized students' need to think critically, participate actively and collaboratively, and build authentic global connections.

The two teachers noted that although the unit addressed the CCR Capacity "Students use technology and digital media strategically and capably" at an elementary level, students' early exposure to authentic tasks and experiences would give them a strong foundation for becoming independent, strategic technology users in the ensuing years.

They finalized their thoughts in Mrs. Cohen's reflective notes:

• **Critical thinking:** Students needed to decide what was important to share with the audience, and each student was tasked with choosing his or her personal destination. The interactive quality of GarageBand heightened their level of engagement and their determination to get their podcast *just right*.

• **Creative problem solving:** Students needed to figure out how to inform others about a destination without the support of images—a complex task for 1st graders, who are used to reading explanatory text and literature that includes images as well as using photographs or drawings to support their own writing.

• **Collaboration:** It was interesting to observe that as students worked in small and large groups on different segments of the writing process and podcast, they were always reminding one another to remember the purpose of writing a script for a listening audience.

- **Communication:** Interacting with people from around the world virtually and immediately was the best part of the culminating experience. Receiving responses from around the world within days rather than weeks (as with the traditional Flat Stanley unit) was the icing on the cake!

- **Technology tools:** Using the interactive whiteboard was meaningful and engaging, enabling students both to hear their voice recordings and to see the audio recordings as visual representations on GarageBand. They also enjoyed exploring world maps online, which truly brought the content alive.

- **Web-based tools:** Using Google Maps on the interactive whiteboard went well. Ms. Taylor's Twitter and blog networking really made a critical difference in the comment results. My new classroom website (maybe I should start a class blog?) is a direct result of upgrading this unit. Finally, students used the Internet to conduct research both in class and at home.

- **Digital storytelling:** We were able to weave new content and prior knowledge into a creative story and used the creative narrative to present information to an audience while simultaneously entertaining it.

- **Media literacy:** The class explored why people create podcasts (e.g., to tell stories, broadcast interviews, and provide information) and learned the components involved in creating one. Students expressed themselves using an online media forum.

- **Writing:** I had never had students write a script before. They (and I) really enjoyed it! The script-writing process included creative and descriptive writing, sequencing, revising, and editing with a specific audience in mind.

- **Speaking/listening:** Students learned the purposeful control of speech focusing on expression for a listening audience. They honed their listening abilities through the podcast recording process and by tweaking the quality of the podcast production.

- **Oral fluency:** Students gained increased awareness of voice, tone, rate, and rhythm and their purpose.

Mrs. Cohen concluded the reflection time by embedding their notations in her unit planner within the district's mapping system for future reference. Ms. Taylor mentioned that she wanted to continue to work together as a transformation team. Because it was only her second year of teaching, being able to observe Mrs. Cohen instructing her students was an invaluable experience. The two teachers arranged a time to meet to discuss a unit to upgrade in both of their classrooms for the next grading period.

Revisions

Later in the school year, Mrs. Cohen discovered the Flat Stanley smartphone application, which enables users to create a virtual Stanley on their phones and take photographs of him or send him to other people. She was also inspired by a video called *Flat Stanley's Hollywood Adventure*, the product of two 2nd graders mailing their Flat Stanley from Illinois to Hollywood. She returned to her reflective notes and added a link to the website (www.flatstanleymovie.com) and noted that for next year's The World Around Us unit, she would have students collaborate to make a video of their Flat Selves visiting areas in their local community, which she would post to TeacherTube and link to the classroom website. This expanded project would address specific social studies standards requirements, including building an awareness of local community life and social interactions.

Discussion Questions

1. What suggestions might you make to help Mrs. Cohen create a deeper, more authentic connection to the English Language Arts CCR Capacity "Students come to understand other perspectives and cultures," keeping in mind her students' age level and cognitive capabilities?

2. During the appraisal and brainstorming phase of the transformation, Ms. Taylor was an important catalyst because of her expertise with technology and web-based tools. When you consider the results of overlapping orbits of ability, why are partnerships so critical for this phase of the transformation spiral?

3. Mrs. Cohen shared some of her planned revisions for The World Around Us. What other revisions might she consider to continue to upgrade this unit?

7

Talk Pals

Transformational Lenses		
Entry Points	**21st Century Clarifications**	**Technology Authenticity**
• Curriculum examinations • Instructional innovations	• Collaborative environments • Global connections	• Web-based tools

Standards Connections
English Language Arts College and Career Readiness Capacities • Students use technology and digital media strategically and capably. • Students come to understand other perspectives and cultures.

Transformational Matrix Upgrade Zone: Outform

Connecting schools around the world is becoming commonplace. What once involved complex procedures now requires just a few simple clicks using web-based tools like videoconferencing and social networking. These interactive venues afford authentic opportunities for students to learn about other cultures and gain perspectives and insights from peers living all over the world.

Traditionally, to make local and global connections, teachers have had students correspond with pen pals abroad. Communicating with others in real time about current events and their locations, traditions, and beliefs is an upgrade that was not possible a few years ago. Providing students with face-to-face opportunities to share information about themselves and their cultures while learning about others' leads to meaningful and authentic learning.

Appraisal and Brainstorming

While attending a conference focused on 21st century classrooms, Ms. Stefani was intrigued by the use of videoconferencing between a 3rd grade class in Florida and a 3rd grade class in Canada. Silvia Rosenthal Tolisano, the presenter of the session on videoconferencing and a 21st century learning specialist in the Florida school, began by sharing a thought: "Technology is not about *replacing* learning or teaching. Technology is a tool to make learning and teaching possible in ways that were never possible before or that we had never imagined."

Mrs. Rosenthal Tolisano then shared her personal experience working with the 3rd grade class to demonstrate how technology and web-based tools enhanced the students' learning experience and helped them make personalized connections to their learning:

> The 3rd graders were going to be reading a historical fiction book, *A Symphony of Whales* by Steve Schuch [2002]. The story describes how the Russian people of Chukchi Peninsula and the crew of the Russian icebreaker ship, *Moskva,* struggled to save thousands of beluga whales trapped by ice in the Siberian Senyavina Strait.
>
> Their teacher asked me if I knew anyone her class could videoconference with who could make the setting of the book, a cold seacoast area rich with whale life, come alive for her students. I immediately turned to my digital learning network on Twitter and sent a tweet to inquire if a 3rd grade class

in Alaska or Canada (since their time zones would work best for meeting with us) could talk to our class about their cold climate, seacoast experiences, and whale life.

Mrs. Heller, a teacher from Port Hardy, British Columbia, was one of the teachers who responded. We set up a Skype videoconference for our two classes that took place soon after our students had read the story and conducted basic research on the Russian geographical area and beluga whales.

When the two classes videoconferenced, it was wonderful to observe the children talking with one another and comparing their ocean-life experiences. Whereas the Canadian class often sees killer whales, our students reported that they do not usually see whales but that they see lots of dolphins, and occasionally sharks.

The two classes compared sea-creature information, such as the size of a whale's tooth versus the size of a shark's tooth found on their respective beaches. Our students also got the opportunity to share what they had learned about beluga whales since the students in Canada had never seen them in the open sea. The most exciting part was that the students' exchange of information did not end there.

Mrs. Heller contacted me via e-mail a few days after the classes had videoconferenced and attached two videos that a student's family had recently taken. During a boat ride, killer whales came close to the stern and appeared to be playing in the boat's wake. Our class was mesmerized and asked us to play the videos over and over again. The students literally jumped out of their seats every time they spotted the whales' large dorsal fins and squealed with delight when the whales arched out of the water.

Our class sent a thank-you tweet to Mrs. Heller's class for videoconferencing and sending the videos, which, they said, took their learning about whales off the page and made it real.

Ms. Stefani, also a 3rd grade teacher, decided that she needed to provide similar opportunities for her students. While recently studying the CCSS for ELA, she and her colleagues had noticed the intensity of the Speaking and Listening standards' expectations. Likewise, they had discussed the CCR Capacities and agreed that they needed to make sure they were nurturing the capacities in their classrooms.

She told her tablemates at the conference session that she was thinking of ways she could incorporate videoconferencing into her classroom that would connect to both the ELA standards and the CCR Capacities. She noted that given her limited expertise with technology tools and web-based software, she was fortunate to have two valuable people in her professional learning community: Mr. Cameron, the school's technology integrator, and Mrs. Richardson, the English as a Second Language (ESL) teacher and a great idea person.

When Ms. Stefani returned to school, she began her transformation process by appraising which of her units she could upgrade to include an authentic application of videoconferencing. She also considered her need to begin revising student learning based on the CCSS for ELA.

At the next professional learning community meeting, Ms. Stefani described Mrs. Rosenthal Tolisano's conference session and told Mr. Cameron and Mrs. Richardson that she would like to meet with them after school one day the following week to discuss upgrading a unit of study. They were intrigued and agreed to the meeting.

At their meeting, Ms. Stefani began by sharing that she had two standards-related curriculum revisions in mind. First, she wanted to incorporate three specific CCSS for ELA Speaking and Listening standards focused on collaborative discussions. Second, she wanted to connect two CCR Capacities—"Students use technology and digital media strategically and capably" and "Students come to understand other perspectives and cultures"—to the state's social studies standards that require students to analyze how local and regional individuals, families, and communities are alike and different. Her students' current method of conducting compare-and-contrast research of local areas (including their own neighborhoods and city as well as other towns and cities in the state) was to read materials they obtained in school, at the library, and online. After hearing about the experiences of Mrs. Rosenthal Tolisano's students, it bothered her that her students never spoke to people throughout their state who knew the information firsthand. She also explained that although her students' grade-level social studies expectations were local (within the state), some of what they learned in other disciplines would be perfect for incorporating authentic global connections.

Mr. Cameron pointed out that videoconferencing would give her students a strong foundation in the meaningful use of technology and web-based tools that would serve them for years to come. Mrs. Richardson added that her ESL students often struggled to make meaningful connections with those living in their state due to their lack of background knowledge. The first- and second-generation Mexican American immigrants with whom she worked had limited English language proficiency as well as different family and cultural traditions from nonimmigrants in their state.

Ms. Stefani nodded in agreement and expressed her desire to achieve a transformation honoring the diversity in her classroom. Although she used a variety of Spanish materials and resources in her classroom and often called on Mrs. Richardson for assistance, she wanted to provide a more personalized, meaningful experience for her Spanish speakers.

They concluded the meeting by agreeing to brainstorm ideas individually and then meet again in a few days to work on upgrading an upcoming unit. As Mr. Cameron and Mrs. Richardson left Ms. Stefani's room, she reminded them that they could view her units easily in their district's mapping system.

Commitment and Communication

When the members of the group reconvened, they discussed possible transformation opportunities based on Ms. Stefani's requisites for the upgrade. Mrs. Richardson had gone online to read more about the CCR Capacities and was inspired by the last sentence in the explanation for the CCR Capacity "Students come to understand other perspectives and cultures" (NGA Center & CCSSO, 2010a):

> Students appreciate that the twenty-first-century classroom and workplace are settings in which people from often widely divergent cultures and who represent diverse experiences and perspectives must learn and work together. Students actively seek to understand other perspectives and cultures through reading and listening, and they are able to communicate effectively with people of varied backgrounds. They evaluate other points of view critically and constructively. *Through reading great classic and contemporary works of literature representative of a variety of periods, cultures, and worldviews, students can vicariously inhabit worlds and have experiences much different than their own.* (p. 7, emphasis added)

After reading this explanation aloud, Mrs. Richardson said, "Although my transformation idea doesn't fully meet your desire to connect this capacity to social studies standards, I think it connects well with both the capacity's requirement to seek to understand other perspectives and cultures through reading and listening and your 3rd graders' literary focus on story elements." She explained that when she had studied Ms. Stefani's upcoming units, one in particular had caught her eye: Fractured Fairy Tales. When she taught this unit in her own class, she said, she enjoyed supporting her ESL students in reading and evaluating traditional fairy tales and alternative versions of the tales—for example, *Little Red Riding Hood* and *Lon Po Po* (Young, 1989). She often found, though, that her students struggled with analyzing the tales, especially the alternative versions, given their language limitations and narrower exposure to traditional fairy tales prior to attending school.

Mrs. Richardson asked Ms. Stefani if she would be interested in having her class videoconference with a class in Spain. Ms. Stefani found the idea intriguing. Mrs. Richardson said that she could ask her friend, Mrs. Ortiz, who taught in a private primary school in Spain, if she would be willing to have her class discuss traditional and alternative fairy tales with peers in the United States.

Mr. Cameron said that this idea reminded him of having pen pals, but because the students' interactions would be oral, they would be *talk pals*. Ms. Stefani loved the term and decided to use it with her students.

Mrs. Richardson said she would need a few days to contact Mrs. Ortiz, with whom she often communicated on Skype. The six-hour time difference meant that setting up a time for the two classes to meet online would take some planning.

Ms. Stefani told Mr. Cameron that she had limited experience with videoconferencing, having only ever observed its use. He suggested that they meet during her students' specials in the next week or two so that he could walk her through setting up a Skype account and help her practice making videoconferencing calls. Mrs. Richardson added that as soon as Ms. Stefani got her account, she would add her as a contact and ask Mrs. Ortiz to add her as well.

About a week later, Mrs. Richardson shared good news: Mrs. Ortiz was enthusiastic about the reading, speaking, and listening videoconferencing opportunities. Mrs. Richardson suggested that she and Ms. Stefani meet with Mrs. Ortiz as soon as possible to discuss the unit's learning focuses and the fairy tales and find natural connections between the learning in both countries. Mrs. Ortiz's biggest concern was the alternative fairy tales, since they might not be popular in Spain.

Early one morning in Florida, Ms. Stefani and Mrs. Richardson videoconferenced with Mrs. Ortiz during her lunch break. After extensive conversation, they decided to pair the classic *The Three Little Pigs* with the contemporary *The True Story of the Three Little Pigs* (Scieszka, 1996).

They scheduled the first Skype session for 8:30 a.m. in Florida, which would be 2:30 p.m. in Spain, and decided that it would focus on *The Three Little Pigs*. The second Skype session, later that week or during the following week, would occur at the same time and focus on the alternative version of the story.

Mrs. Ortiz shared that she had never read *The True Story of the Three Little Pigs*. During the initial videoconference, as they discussed the story, she found a Spanish version online to purchase, *¡La Verdadera Historia de los Tres Cerditos!* The teachers concluded their conversation by discussing what both classes would be learning about plot, a story element that Ms. Stefani wanted to be a key focus of the students' conversations.

Because the Fractured Fairy Tales unit was not taking place for another month, they had the necessary time to prepare individually and collaboratively for the unit. They took the following steps:

• Mrs. Richardson contacted Mrs. Ortiz to set up specific dates for the two videoconferencing sessions based on Ms. Stefani's students' progress in learning about the two fairy tales.

• Ms. Stefani spoke to her principal, Mr. Douglass, about the need for her students to miss a special on the second day they were planning to videoconference with the Spanish students.

• Mr. Douglass asked Ms. Stefani to send home permission slips with her students asking guardians to grant permission for their children to participate in an audiovisual exchange. Mrs. Richardson translated the permission form into Spanish to ensure that all parents and caregivers had a clear understanding of the permission's intent.

• Mr. Douglass, intrigued by the unit upgrade, said that he would like to attend the videoconferencing sessions. Ms. Stefani confided to him that she felt a bit nervous about the upgrade, considering her limited comfort level with technology and her students' varying language abilities, but shared that she believed the potential for engaging her students in a meaningful way was worth her uneasiness.

• Mr. Cameron ensured that both classes were technologically prepared for the Skype sessions and tested their videoconference capabilities on the days prior to both videoconferences.

In preparation for the first Skype session, Ms. Stefani's class learned about the same aspects of *The Three Little Pigs* that her previous classes had studied, including plot—a new term and concept for the 3rd graders. The difference was that they knew they would be discussing this fairy tale's story elements with their talk pals in another country. They used Google Earth to locate Spain on their interactive whiteboard, with the aid of Mr. Cameron. They zoomed in on and virtually toured the town where their talk pals lived. Their excitement grew when they saw the front of the school building where they knew their talk pals were reading the same story.

They discussed five questions related to the fairy tale that Ms. Stefani and Mrs. Ortiz had come up with together, including "What do you think is the most important event in this fairy tale's plot?" Next, they thought of a bonus question about the story to ask their talk pals.

During the first videoconferencing session, Mrs. Richardson was on hand to interpret when necessary. After making their introductions, Ms. Stefani read the first half of the story in English and Mrs. Ortiz read the second half in Spanish. The two classes then participated in a discussion of the fairy tale's characters, setting, and plot based on the five questions.

When it was time to ask the bonus question, Ms. Stefani's students were excited. One of her students asked the question: "If you were the author and could change the story's ending, what would you have happen?" Another student in Ms. Stefani's class then asked the question in Spanish. Mrs. Ortiz gave her students a few minutes to brainstorm their responses and then had them share their responses. One of Mrs. Ortiz's students shared his response in English: "I make the ending be where Wolf became friends with the pigs."

Before they said goodbye, Ms. Stefani and Mrs. Ortiz held up the alternative version of the fairy tale and shared that they were excited about meeting again in a week to discuss the *true* story. After the session concluded, Ms. Stefani's class was abuzz with English and Spanish conversation about their talk pals experience. Some students mentioned that their talk pals' ideas for different endings were the same ones they had come up with when they wrote their own endings.

The second videoconferencing session was as enjoyable as the first session. This time, Mrs. Ortiz's students asked the bonus question: "¿Si usted fuera el juez del Lobo le creería usted su cuento?" Mrs. Richardson translated: "If you were the Wolf's judge, would you believe his story?" Ms. Stefani gave her students time to brainstorm their answers. Some shared their thoughts with Mrs. Ortiz's class in English (for example, "I would only believe the Wolf if I met his granny"), and a few students responded in Spanish. When it was time to say their goodbyes, a few of

Ms. Stefani's students became teary-eyed. After the call concluded, the first question students asked was when they were going to get to work with their talk pals again.

Reactions and Reflections

Soon after the conclusion of the unit, Ms. Stefani asked Mr. Cameron and Mrs. Richardson to meet with her to debrief the unit while it was still fresh in their minds. Although they all agreed that the unit achieved the intended expectations, Ms. Stefani believed there was room for improvement, especially related to the CCSS for ELA that she had wanted to make an explicit part of the unit's learning.

The collaborative discussions within her class and with Mrs. Ortiz's class had been engaging and respectful, but she felt she needed to work more deliberately to help her students exhibit behaviors associated with the ELA Speaking and Listening standards, such as the ability to restate what someone else shared before adding one's own thoughts. She realized that the transformation had truly engaged her class in ways that had never happened when she taught this unit in the past, but that the learning had not really changed. Although she had been aware of students' behaviors during their collaborative discussions, she had not formally assessed any discussions or used a rubric to guide students in evaluating the quality of their own participation in the discussions.

Mr. Cameron created a collaborative Google Doc to allow the group to add additional thoughts and suggestions for revision in the coming months. Some of their thoughts included the following:

- **Communication:** Our students interacted with their classmates with a new level of engagement knowing that they were going to be conversing with talk pals. They were even more conscientious about this before and during the second video-conferencing session. Their conversation based on the planned questions went well, and it was fun to watch them respond to the impromptu questions. Although the two classes understood each other pretty well in English and Spanish, it was beneficial to have Mrs. Richardson there to interpret when needed.
- **Speaking and listening:** The students had to be cognizant of their pace and volume when speaking in English to the Spanish class to avoid misunderstanding. It was interesting to see that our students' word choice became more thoughtful to aid the Spanish students' understanding. In addition, our Mexican American

students listened carefully as Mrs. Ortiz read portions of the fairy tales in Spanish since there were nuances in her accent that they were not familiar with. Both our native English speakers and our Mexican American students were helpful when anyone (in either class) needed help in comprehending what was said.

• **Reading:** Knowing that they were going to be conversing with their talk pals, our students focused on the story elements with excitement. Most interesting was that when we discussed the five questions and outlined our talking points for the alternative fairy tale, they showed increased thoughtfulness in their responses and in contemplating what the Spanish students would say, due to having built personal connections with these students across the globe who were also learning about fairy tales and story elements.

• **Web-based tools:** Videoconferencing using Skype made a world of difference (no pun intended). Both classes interacted visually—with each student introducing him- or herself in camera view during the first session—as well as orally, with Mr. Cameron walking around with a portable camera to ensure that our students could be seen and heard throughout the sessions. During the second session, one of our students noticed Skype's chat feature and asked if we could type a question in the box. Writing the question in this manner added an unexpected literacy dynamic.

• **Global connections:** Students got firsthand experience interacting with their peers in another country. It was interesting for the two classes to explore similarities and differences in their thoughts about the fairy tales—not only those we read and discussed for the unit but also additional fairy tales brought up in response to an impromptu question posed by one of our students.

Mr. Douglass joined the meeting and said that he had enjoyed attending both videoconferencing sessions. The teachers shared their notes, and Ms. Stefani discussed the improvements she would like to make to more fully incorporate the Speaking and Listening standards.

Revisions

As summertime approached, Ms. Stefani, Mrs. Richardson, and Mr. Cameron met for an end-of-year discussion on continuing to upgrade the Fractured Fairy Tales unit for the next school year.

Ms. Stefani mentioned that she would be attending a workshop focused on the CCSS for ELA during the summer that emphasized the Speaking and Listening standards. She hoped the presenters would either provide or help attendees create discussion rubrics that she could use to improve her ability to teach and assess her students' discussion and questioning skills. Mr. Cameron suggested contacting Mrs. Rosenthal Tolisano to ask if she had any insights on creating discussion rubrics. Ms. Stefani liked the idea and made a note of it.

Mrs. Richardson suggested adding a third videoconferencing session as a culminating experience. Each class could independently vote on a favorite fairy tale from its respective country and read the tale aloud to the other class during a videoconference called *Our Reading Corner (Nuestro Rincón de Lectura)*. Ms. Stefani said she had recently heard about grandparents reading to their grandchildren via Skype and suggested that the two classes could have a student's grandparent read the favorite fairy tale during the third videoconferencing session.

Mr. Cameron came up with another idea: having the two classes jointly write an original fairy tale and read it during the culminating experience. He explained that the classes could take turns writing sections of their book online using Storybird, a web-based collaborative storytelling tool. He elaborated, "For example, Ms. Stefani's class could write the beginning. Mrs. Ortiz's class would then write the first half of the middle, Ms. Stefani's class would write the second half of the middle, and Mrs. Ortiz's class would write the ending." He pointed out that because the classes could access Storybird at any time, they could write the book collaboratively without needing to add more videoconferencing sessions. Based on decisions the two classes would make during the first two videoconferencing sessions regarding their fairy tale's characters, setting, and plot, he could monitor their developing book in Storybird and let each class know when the other class had completed a particular section. The classes would also be able to conduct peer reviews, leaving each other suggestions for revision or concerns in the comment box for the book.

Both Mrs. Richardson and Ms. Stefani liked the idea of adding a collaborative writing component to their students' interactions and agreed that this potential revision to the unit could lead to the desired transformation. First, though, they needed to find out whether Mrs. Ortiz was willing to continue her partnership in talk pals and participate in the plans for the new transformation.

When they videoconferenced with Mrs. Ortiz a few days later, she liked their new ideas and was willing to spend some time working on the new transformation over the summer with Ms. Stefani and Mrs. Richardson. After the videoconference, Mr. Cameron added that he thought Ms. Stefani's class could become more hands-on in conducting the videoconferencing sessions and offered to come up with roles students could play prior to and during the Skype sessions. The teachers concluded their meeting by adding their revisions to the Google Doc they had created for the unit earlier in the school year.

Discussion Questions

1. Three teachers with different orbits of ability came together to brainstorm, implement, reflect on, and revise an upgraded unit of study: a general education teacher, an ESL teacher, and a technology integrator. How did these teachers' varied areas of expertise benefit the transformational process? What web-based tools might your transformation team choose to support collaboration, communication, and documentation?

2. Mr. Cameron pointed out during the debriefing session that Ms. Stefani's students had not had any difficulties using the classroom technology or Skype features. One of the CCR Capacities calls for students to use technology *capably*. What suggestions do you have to make Ms. Stefani's class videoconferencing sessions more student-led?

3. Take a few moments to analyze the similarities and differences between Mrs. Rosenthal Tolisano's upgrade from the beginning of the chapter and Ms. Stefani's upgrade. Are they both *outform* upgrades? Explain your reasoning.

8

Microloans:
A Glocal Impact

Transformational Lenses		
Entry Points	21st Century Clarifications	Technology Authenticity
• Performance task assessments • Curriculum examinations • Instructional innovations	• Higher-order thinking • Global connections • Glocal impacts	• Web-based tools

Standards Connections
English Language Arts College and Career Readiness Capacities • Students build strong content knowledge. • Students respond to the varying demands of audience, task, purpose, and discipline. • Students value evidence. • Students use technology and digital media strategically and capably. • Students come to understand other perspectives and cultures. *Standards for Mathematical Practice* • Construct viable arguments and critique the reasoning of others.

Transformational Matrix Upgrade Zone: Transform

Microloans are small, short-term loans made to impoverished entrepreneurs in underdeveloped countries. During the early 21st century, microloan services have changed from being offline ventures funded by banks to becoming online ventures that can be funded by anyone. An investor commits a small amount of money—for example, $25—which, when combined with other investors' microloans, provides enough funds to support an entrepreneur's proposal. Once the loan is paid back, an investor may choose to fund a new proposal or withdraw from investing.

Using microloans as an educational opportunity for project-based learning is gaining popularity. It provides an authentic way to connect multiple content areas, such as social studies, English language arts, mathematics, and financial literacy.

Mr. Pruitt, a 7th grade teacher of English language arts and social studies, initially upgraded his geography-based unit by incorporating global connections. As time passed and he observed students' reactions and listened to their concerns and frustrations, he decided to upgrade the unit again to involve glocal impacts.

Appraisal and Brainstorming

Mr. Pruitt became aware of videoconferencing as a free web-based tool approximately two years ago and recognized that this tool could help connect his students to places and people that state standards required them to learn about. Videoconferencing would enable his students to explore the culture, economics, and everyday life of locations they studied that they may never physically visit.

To get more information on videoconferencing as an instructional innovation, he began to connect virtually with educators using Twitter and educational social networking sites like Teachers Recess (www.teachersrecess.com).

While planning for his upcoming units of study, Mr. Pruitt contacted educators in India, China, and Australia who were willing to videoconference at odd hours to converse with his class during school hours. He had his students prepare for the sessions by researching the country or continent the class was studying. During the videoconference, students would ascertain whether their findings were accurate. For each unit, he divided students into small teams to research political, social, economic, and cultural statistics.

The videoconferencing sessions went well, but he noticed that student engagement, initially high, began to wane during the third unit's preparation and videoconference session. When he surveyed his class, he found that students had valid complaints:

- The time-zone differences meant they were interviewing adults rather than their peers.
- They weren't learning about what truly interested them, like current events, music, and famous people. Instead, they were limited to asking questions about daily life, the economy, and social structures.
- They didn't get the opportunity to work collaboratively with people from the countries they were connecting with.

Mr. Pruitt told his students that although there was nonnegotiable content they needed to learn, he understood their frustrations. In particular, he was interested by their last concern and promised to investigate the possibilities of securing more-authentic interactions.

He shared his recent class experience, concerns, and goals with a few educators via Twitter and received various responses. A few responses that mentioned *micro-lending* caught his eye. He researched this concept and became intrigued with what he found.

Commitment and Communication

Mr. Pruitt shared his idea for upgrading his unit with a few colleagues in his school and asked if they, too, would be interested in getting their students involved in microloan investments. Although the teachers shared his enthusiasm and agreed that the upgrade would align with a standards-based curriculum, he could not find anyone willing to commit to the upgrade.

While Mr. Pruitt was researching microlending opportunities, he remembered that he had received a gift certificate to use at Kiva from Mr. McHolms, a social-network colleague who had integrated microloan investments into his students' curriculum. He contacted Mr. McHolms to learn more and read the "About Micro-finance" page on Kiva's (n.d.) website:

> Microfinance is a general term to describe financial services to low-income individu-als or to those who do not have access to typical banking services.

Microfinance is also the idea that low-income individuals are capable of lifting themselves out of poverty if given access to financial services. While some studies indicate that microfinance can play a role in the battle against poverty, it is also recognized that it is not always the appropriate method, and that it should never be seen as the only tool for ending poverty. (paras. 1–2)

Mr. McHolms explained further how Kiva worked:

• Prospective borrowers create summaries of their needs and reasons for the loan and post on the website.

• Lenders decide whom they want to finance and invest online in increments starting at $25. The money is sent to an intermediary bank that handles the lenders' and borrowers' monetary transactions.

• Borrowers pay back their lenders once their increased incomes allow.

• Lenders, once repaid, may choose to invest with new borrowers or not reinvest.

Mr. Pruitt realized that having his students become lenders would align well to specific social studies, mathematics, reading, writing, and research standards. In addition, making microloans in countries they were required to learn about would engage them in higher-order thinking and decision making. He was most excited about this transformation's authentic connection to recently implemented standards for financial literacy.

He decided to design a microloan-themed project-based assessment for an upcoming unit of study on Africa. He knew committing to this project meant transforming not only the curriculum but also his instruction. Because he could not find a colleague at his school willing to work with him on the upgrade, he contacted Mr. McHolms, who agreed to collaborate and communicate with Mr. Pruitt via e-mail, Twitter, and, when necessary, Skype.

Mr. Pruitt spent two weeks planning for the necessary adjustments. He first talked with his principal to make sure it was permissible for his students to be involved in loaning money. His principal told him they could as long as the actual funds came from Mr. Pruitt's Kiva account. Mr. Pruitt had received a $75 check from a friend to use for the microloan unit, bringing his investment funds to a total of $100.

Mr. Pruitt introduced the unit by posting its overarching question: "What can we do locally that will have an impact globally?" He explained to students that in this unit, they would be participating in a culminating project-based assessment requiring them to provide microloans to borrowers in Africa and write persuasive pieces explaining their rationales for choosing their borrowers. He explained the concept of glocal impacts and pointed out that by connecting glocally, students would forge a more personal connection to the unit and its subject matter—something they had felt was lacking in the earlier units integrating global connections.

During the next few days of instruction, Mr. Pruitt introduced his students to the Kiva website. Because the class was currently studying Africa, students were only to consider borrowers from this continent. In addition, they must make loans to individuals, not groups. He showed them how to use the filtering features on the Kiva website to narrow down potential borrowers to individuals and locate desired loan categories, such as agriculture, retail, services, and transportation.

Mr. Pruitt divided the class into four collaborative teams, with each team receiving $25 for its microloan investment. He began to gradually release the students from large-group instruction to work in their teams to investigate potential borrowers. He gave them guiding questions to increase their learning and awareness and to foster higher-order thinking:

Will your team lend to a male or female?

• What will the social or cultural impact be on the borrower's family or village if you choose a female over a male? A male over a female?

• What do current data reveal about lending to a woman who wants to do work outside what is socially accepted in her culture?

• What do current data reveal about lending to a man who wants to do work outside what is socially accepted in his culture?

• What cultural values do you need to understand before making a decision about whom to lend to?

To what extent may the individual and his or her group, village, or community benefit from your team's microloan?

• What will have the greatest positive impact: an agricultural microloan? A retail microloan? A services microloan? A transportation microloan?

• How many people will ultimately be positively impacted by your choice?

What factors in the regions you are considering investing in does your team need to consider (for example, ancestral traditions, current traditions, current governmental practices and requirements, and/or civil unrest or war)?

- How are ancestral and current local traditions affecting your selection of potential borrowers?
- What do current data reveal about loan-risk assessments (the risk associated with the probability that a given loan would be repaid) in the country where your potential borrower lives?
- What do current data reveal about possible government control or influence in opposing the legality of receiving or paying back the loan?
- How would you feel if the loan is never repaid? Based on your reasons for lending to your chosen borrower, how does this affect your decision making?

Students spent class time researching and discussing their responses to the probing questions. They also worked outside class, with each team member delegated to investigate specific aspects of the questions. Mr. Pruitt facilitated the investigation process by circulating throughout the classroom to discuss answers to the posed questions and clarify confusions that arose. For example, as one team explored whether to loan to a male or female, Mr. Pruitt explained that in some African cultures, a woman who wanted to start an industrial business—such as sewing clothes rather than doing the acceptable agricultural job of raising goats—would be looked down on for doing what was traditionally perceived as men's work. This discussion eventually opened up to involve all four teams, and they conducted a comparative analysis of acceptable women's jobs and roles in the United States versus those in various African countries.

To keep the videoconferencing sessions engaging and meaningful, once each team had narrowed down its potential borrowers to two, Mr. Pruitt arranged videoconferences with teachers who lived and worked in the country or countries where the potential candidates lived. Each team could then ask specific, strategic questions based on its research that added a global collaborative aspect to the decision-making process. The teams also read informational texts online and incorporated the data they found into persuasive summaries stating who would receive their $25 microloans and how they had reached their decisions.

The students' engagement was immediate and evident throughout the unit. After the teams made their microloans, one student announced, "We may have not changed the world, but we just changed someone's life."

Reactions and Reflections

Investing in microloans gave Mr. Pruitt's students the ability to make authentic global connections and glocal impacts. His students felt personally invested in their learning. Whereas in his earlier units they had used videoconferencing to ask questions about a country, in this unit his students had engaged in more meaningful interactions.

During a debriefing videoconferencing session with Mr. McHolms, Mr. Pruitt shared some of his students' reactions and his own reflections. He noted that his students now had more than a general knowledge of people living in faraway places; they had an intimate, focused understanding of specific people and of real issues that were affecting these people's daily lives and, in some cases, their survival.

He explained that much of what had happened during the unit had been part of his plan, but that the impromptu instruction and discussion inspired by the unit had made the transformation even more meaningful for him.

Mr. Pruitt later recorded some of the most pertinent reflections in a Microsoft Word document:

• **Critical thinking:** Students had to weigh the risks associated with making a loan. They actively discussed pros and cons involving cultural values and local traditions to make their ultimate decisions. They researched multiple information sources, conducted videoconference interviews, and synthesized the data to draw their conclusions.

• **Collaboration:** Each team truly worked as a unit. Students held themselves accountable for answering the guiding questions about potential borrowers, especially as they analyzed the borrowers' summaries and the potential positive and negative implications of each investment. Each team reached a consensus on the borrower it invested in and worked collaboratively to generate a meaningful, persuasive summary explaining why the investment in its chosen candidate was worthwhile.

• **Global connections:** Students had the opportunity to authentically verify their investigative research while videoconferencing with the teachers (local experts) from the countries where their potential borrowers lived.

• **Web-based tools:** Although students used the Kiva website as their initial source of information, they supplemented their learning using simple and advanced searches, wikis, and online encyclopedias. Each team also created a LiveBinder (www.livebinders.com) that helped them organize and curate the information they found and communicated using TodaysMeet (www.todaysmeet.com) as an online discussion tool.

• **Technology tools:** Students were already well versed in using the interactive whiteboard. They found this tool useful for sharing the latest information in their Live-Binders both within teams and during whole-class discussions. They also used word-processing software to write their persuasive essays and organize their note taking.

• **Writing:** Students used persuasive techniques to convince their audience (i.e., their peer teams) that they had made the right decisions regarding their choice of borrower. Using a persuasive-writing rubric tweaked by the class enabled all the students to engage in evaluating each team's persuasive writing. Honestly, they were harder on themselves than I would have been! I think because they were so invested in the decision-making process, they took each team's reasoning very seriously, which deepened the quality of their writing.

Before concluding the debriefing session, Mr. Pruitt shared one more experience with Mr. McHolms. He had decided to try to reconnect with a former student who had exhibited frequent behavior problems and poor attendance. He asked the student to join him for lunch. While they were eating, he asked, "Would you be interested in positively impacting someone's life right now?" After asking a few questions, the student said he would be interested. Mr. Pruitt showed him the Kiva website, and they took some time browsing it and looking at its features. Mr. Pruitt then showed the student the guiding questions his students had used to determine which borrowers they would invest in. The student asked to take a copy of the questions. Over the next few days, he stopped by Mr. Pruitt's room after school to update him on his investigations. In about a week's time, he came to Mr. Pruitt's room and sat down, looking quite serious. He shared that he was ready to invest $25 of his own money to help a borrower in Uganda start a transportation business. The Ugandan man currently worked for someone who was taking 50 percent of his daily earnings away from him and needed to purchase a bicycle to start his own business. The student believed that this man would be a good investment. As Mr. Pruitt shared with Mr. McHolms, this young man's commitment really made his day!

Revisions

Near the end of the school year, during a lesson that involved reading a world map, Mr. Pruitt noticed that his students immediately turned their attention to the locations where they had provided microloans, making comments like "I wonder how many people were impacted by the animals that Moumine purchased to sell in the local market. We need to remember to check on our borrowers' profiles over the summer." Mr. Pruitt knew that his educational investment had paid off and that embedding microloans into the learning experience had been a worthwhile transformation. He made a mental note to teach a microloans-based unit early the following school year so that his students could keep track of their investments and, with luck, be paid back before the end of the school year.

Although Mr. Pruitt was pleased with the results of the microloan project-based assessment, he knew there were a few design aspects that he needed to modify for the next academic year. For example, now that he had had more training in the CCSS for ELA, he knew his students needed to learn to write effective arguments, including formal claims and opposing claims, rather than traditional persuasive pieces.

Another modification he needed to make would be based on the CCSS for ELA Speaking and Listening standards. As part of his professional learning community's focus for the upcoming school year, his grade-level team discussed creating a rubric to measure how well the content and skills aligned with the first Speaking and Listening standard: "Engage effectively in a range of collaborative discussions (one-on-one, in groups, and teacher-led) with diverse partners on grade 7 topics, texts, and issues, building on others' ideas and expressing their own clearly." Mr. Pruitt would be able to use this rubric to have his students evaluate their own and their peers' persuasive pieces as they worked collaboratively during the microloan-themed unit.

In addition, Mr. Pruitt noted that he wanted the next unit to better apply the Standard for Mathematical Practice "Construct viable arguments and critique the reasoning of others." He decided to have his incoming students pay closer attention to connections among mathematical evidence-based sources, such as interpreting various data to help them determine the worthiness of a particular loan, as they research potential borrowers. In an e-mail to Mr. McHolms, he noted that this standard aligned well with the CCSS requirement to construct quality arguments. He observed that this mathematics–English language arts connection would help students understand that although the term *argument* may have multiple meanings, the concept and process behind creating an argument remain the same across different contexts.

In the course of continued conversations with teachers in his DLN who used the Kiva website, Mr. Pruitt discovered that many had expanded their classroom use of Kiva to start schoolwide Microloan Clubs. Many clubs created an initial $500 school portfolio to fund microloans and continued to fundraise throughout the year to increase their opportunities to make glocal impacts. He liked this idea and planned to investigate the possibilities in his school with some of his colleagues.

Mr. Pruitt also learned about organizations other than Kiva that conducted or supported similar investments and projects. With ongoing changes in the curriculum and standards in his state, he was glad to be able to take advantage of other nonprofits' offerings to expand authentic opportunities to make global connections and glocal impacts in his class and, potentially, the entire school.

To continue to gain new insights and communicate virtually with educators around the world, he became a member of globally connected educational websites like Around the World with 80 Schools (www.aroundtheworldwith80schools.net) and Skype in the Classroom (education.skype.com).

Discussion Questions

1. What are some potential immediate or future implications of Mr. Pruitt's colleagues choosing not to upgrade their units along with him? How might their choices affect equity of learning and teaching in the school? What might you suggest as a positive first step toward encouraging teachers to participate collaboratively in transformations?

2. Mr. Pruitt used videoconferencing in a previous transformation. At first, the tool engaged students, but it lost its impact after a while. The revised upgrade involving microloan services made the videoconferencing sessions more authentic and meaningful for students. If student interest in the microloan aspect of the unit begins to wane, however, what suggestions might you offer to help Mr. Pruitt spiral though another transformation?

3. The standards connections in the transformational lenses table include the CCR Capacity that requires students to respond to the varying demands of audience, task, purpose, and discipline. What evidence in this snapshot supports this particular lens? Can you suggest ways to increase the infusion of this capacity in a microloans-based unit of study?

9

Film Festival

Transformational Lenses		
Entry Points	**21st Century Clarifications**	**Technology Authenticity**
• Performance task assessments • Culminating experiences • Curriculum examinations • Instructional innovations	• Higher-order thinking • Local connections	• Technology tools • Web-based tools
Standards Connections		
English Language Arts College and Career Readiness Capacities • Students demonstrate independence. • Students respond to the varying demands of audience, task, purpose, and discipline. • Students comprehend as well as critique. • Students use technology and digital media strategically and capably.		
Transformational Matrix Upgrade Zone: Transform		

During the summer of 2010, shortly after the release of the CCSS for ELA, a district consisting of four elementary schools, one middle school, and one high school convened a collaborative task force to design a set of districtwide Essential Maps for K–12 English language arts curriculum. The task force included 35 teachers, the assistant superintendent, and the ELA curriculum coordinator, Mrs. Jodi.

During the process of breaking down the CCSS for ELA, the middle school and high school teachers on the task force noticed requisites that were not in the current state standards. Students would be expected to compare, contrast, analyze, and evaluate a text and multimedia versions of that text, including film productions. The members of the task force believed that to be an astute reader or viewer, one must also be a writer. As a result, when they designed the vertically articulated curriculum for middle school through high school, they included a screenplay-writing unit in the 8th grade. The unit would help students build an understanding of the characteristics of the film genre, the screenplay format, the importance of setting and plot, and characterization. The assessment for the unit would require students to use the writing process to collaboratively develop screenplays.

Appraisal and Brainstorming

Although the state had officially adopted the CCSS, it did not expect school districts to immediately align curriculum to the standards for the following school year. However, teachers in this district were required to teach the units of study laid out in the newly developed ELA Essential Maps. Mrs. Jodi visited schools in the district on a rotating basis throughout the year to aid teachers in their implementation. Some units whose requisites were based heavily on the CCSS rather than current state standards would likely be challenging to teach. Mrs. Jodi visited the district's middle school toward the end of the school year and met with the English department. She commented that no 8th grade class had yet undertaken the screenplay-writing unit. When she asked why, the teachers replied that with everything else they needed to teach for current state testing, there was simply not enough time.

Mr. Nations, who had been a member of the district's ELA task force, acknowledged that this unit was necessary, especially considering what the students would be expected to know and be able to do next year in high school. He explained that he and another teacher in the English department, Ms. Keeley, had recently been discussing this unit and agreed that it would not be truly effective if the students did not actually produce films based on their screenplays. Ms. Keeley added that they were concerned that they had never before taught students how to write a screenplay, so their own learning curve would be considerable. Mrs. Jodi told the teachers that she appreciated their honesty. After returning to her office, she consulted with the assistant superintendent, and they both agreed that this particular unit would not be required for the current school year. Mrs. Jodi informed the high school English department that the middle school would work toward including the screenplay-writing unit in the next academic year.

Commitment and Communication

In the middle of the following school year, Mrs. Jodi again visited the middle school and asked the teachers in the English department about the screenplay-writing unit. Although the 8th grade teachers expressed the same concerns they had the previous year, they informed Mrs. Jodi that they would be teaching the unit this year; they just hadn't yet determined when they would teach it. With Mrs. Jodi, they discussed options for when and how they would teach the unit.

After Mrs. Jodi's visit, Mr. Nations and Ms. Keeley decided to prepare for and teach the unit as a team near the end of the school year. Their first thought was that the students would need to have an audience to view their film productions, so they decided to hold a film festival as a culminating experience. Although they had no idea what a film festival would involve, they knew it was the right choice to make the unit authentic and purposeful. Once they started researching the processes of writing screenplays and producing films, they decided that the screenplay-writing and film production unit would take approximately seven weeks. Knowing they wanted the film festival to correspond with the end of the school year, they worked backward to determine when the unit would begin.

During the months following Mrs. Jodi's visit, they periodically worked on planning the unit, which took more time than they had anticipated. The most time-consuming aspects of the preparation turned out to be

- Determining an appropriate instructional sequence.
- Locating helpful websites for students to use during the unit.

- Researching premade rubrics as well as creating their own.
- Developing formative and summative assessments.
- Obtaining cameras (e.g., Flip cameras, digital cameras) for filming.
- Planning the specifics of the film festival.

They set a strong focus on ensuring that higher-order thinking played a significant role in the unit. They wanted students to

- Culminate their middle school experience with a performance task that required them to incorporate knowledge and skills they had attained during the last three years.
- Apply analytical skills and strategies and consider audience, task, and purpose while writing, revising, filming, and editing their productions.
- Work collaboratively to develop a reality-based storyline and bring it to life using actors, settings, camera angles, lighting, and music that reflected the storyline.
- Apply technology and web-based tools effectively and strategically throughout the unit and for the performance task.

The most significant personal learning curve for Mr. Nations and Ms. Keeley was teaching themselves the art and process of filmmaking. Neither the middle school nor the high school offered a film course, and the middle school fine arts teacher did not know the specifics of film production. They realized the process would require students to synthesize their reading and viewing experiences, become adept at literary and media analysis, and learn about literary elements and devices, screenplay format, and film production. They wanted the unit's filmmaking procedure to be as accurate and authentic as possible.

Before beginning the unit, Mr. Nations and Ms. Keeley discussed the logistics of dividing students into collaborative teams. The school's three-day rotating ABC schedule would actually support the unit's needs. Mr. Nations taught writing for 45 minutes in his room while Ms. Keeley taught reading in her room, and then the sections switched. This would mean that the student teams could work collaboratively for a total of 90 minutes each day.

At the onset of the unit, Mr. Nations and Ms. Keeley outlined the expectations for the screenplay-writing, film production, and culminating film festival segments of the unit to both sections (8A and 8B). They showed the students how to access the Film Festival wiki they had created on Wikispaces that contained downloadable handouts and rubrics, links to online resources, and a TodaysMeet meeting room to use as a collaborative communication tool.

Each student received a permission letter to take home stating that his or her class would be examining scenes from scripts that the teachers had found online and viewing the corresponding scene clips. The films included three PG-rated films (*Elf, Jaws,* and *Rocky*); two PG-13-rated films (*Avatar* and *The Lord of the Rings: The Fellowship of the Ring*); and one R-rated film (*Sleepy Hollow*). The letter read,

> Over the next several weeks, the 8th grade reading and writing classes will be working on a collaborative unit grounded in the study of cinema. This unit requires students to write, direct, film, and edit a team-created short film. Students will use critical reading and writing skills to create a visual product that evokes an intended reaction from their viewers.
>
> In order for students to be successful, they need to study films before embarking on a production of their own. In an effort to present your child with a valuable learning experience based on the study of film, Ms. Keeley and Mr. Nations have selected clips from the indicated films. Please note that some of the scenes may contain mild violence, but only grade-appropriate scenes will be shown and studied.
>
> While we believe that studying film is powerful and educational, we respect your views as parents/guardians. Should you not want your child to view any of these film clips, please contact us by calling or e-mailing, and we will make alternative arrangements for your child. If you have any questions or concerns, please feel free to contact us.

The permission letter required a signature from a parent or guardian. No one opted out of the unit.

For the first two weeks of the unit, Mr. Nations focused on teaching students the process of developing a script from an existing book versus developing a script from original story ideas. The students studied scripts and screenplays to determine the differences between the two and wrote short scene segments in both formats after they learned more about screenplay elements like formatting (e.g., blocking text, action indications, lighting directions, writing in present tense even if the storyline includes flashbacks), developing characters, writing conversational dialogue, and expressing emotion through dialogue and stage direction.

During these initial two weeks, Ms. Keeley had students read and analyze sections of each selected film's screenplay. After the students examined a section, they viewed the corresponding film scene to gain an understanding of how written text is translated onto the screen. For example, Ms. Keeley used the main character in *Elf*, Buddy, to model how a particular character is developed. She used a scene in *Jaws* to express the concept of *mood* and to convey the idea that film can create suspense without taking violence to an extreme. She facilitated a discussion on how lighting, camera angles, purposeful music, and sound effects can evoke emotions in a film's viewers.

At the beginning of the third week, both teachers concentrated on the history and evolution of Hollywood cinema. Mr. Nations's students explored how changes in the film industry, including technological advances, influenced screenplay writing. Ms. Keeley facilitated discussions on popular film genres, including action, adventure, comedy, drama, horror, science fiction, and romance. She gave the students a genre quiz to make certain they were equipped with a common understanding of each genre and its characteristics. Because the students would receive a final grade in both classes, keeping track of the formative and summative assessments throughout the unit was a joint effort. Mr. Nations and Ms. Keeley met every day after school to make sure that what was taking place in both classrooms was cohesive and discussed any issues or concerns that arose.

Midweek, students began to use the majority of time in both classes to work in collaborative teams to write their screenplays and plan the filming of their productions. With two sections of approximately 20 students each, Mr. Nations and Ms. Keeley planned to divide students into six teams of six to seven students, but they wanted students' preferences to influence the makeup of the teams. The teachers asked each student to complete a Film Team Form with two components. The first part asked the student to list approximately five students with whom he or she would like to work, and the second part asked the student to indicate his or her favorite film genre. The teachers reviewed the forms, assembled the teams accordingly, and posted the team rosters on the Film Festival wiki.

Next, it was time to determine team members' roles. Each team needed one director, two scriptwriters, two Flip-camera operators, and one or two film editors who needed to be familiar with iMovie, the filmmaking program used in the unit. Each team nominated its director. This was the only role heavily influenced by Mr. Nations and Ms. Keeley, since they knew their students' personalities and ability to work (or not work) collaboratively in a leadership capacity. The remaining roles were determined at each team's discretion. In addition to fulfilling these roles, every team member was expected to be an actor as well as a reviewer, reviser, and editor of the screenplay and film production.

Before the teams selected their themes, Mr. Nations and Ms. Keeley announced that teams would not be permitted to create zombie or horror films, even though these were the most popular genres listed on students' Film Team Forms. The teachers reminded the students that the film festival audience might include young (or young-at-heart) viewers who would find these genres disturbing.

Each team received two handouts—Grade 8 Film Project Expectations and Film Stages Checklist—that listed the deadlines for each stage and would aid teams in tracking their progress. In addition, each team received a Video Project Rubric that outlined how its final product would be assessed. The teams worked independently, with Mr. Nations and Ms. Keeley facilitating in their respective classrooms, consulting with teams at each stage of the writing and film production process, and providing additional help as needed. Some students chose to work in the library, which had better Internet access than the classrooms did. Students uploaded their work to the Film Festival wiki when appropriate, which aided the teachers in monitoring the teams' progress. On occasion, Mr. Nations or Ms. Keeley would explain the details or requirements for a particular next step to the entire class in their respective classrooms, since all of the teams worked at roughly the same pace.

During the writing and film production stages, Mr. Nations and Ms. Keeley conducted formative assessments and informal class discussions. They based the final assessment on each team's final 10- to15-minute film production, which was expected to represent the culmination of the collaborative work outlined in the Video Project Rubric. Although the teachers determined each team's final grade, they took into consideration each team's evaluation of its own film as well as the scores given by the rest of the classmates.

The stages of the writing and production process included movie proposal, storyboard/screenplay script, filming, film editing/final production, film poster, and film festival.

Movie proposal. Each team came up with a name for its production company and submitted an e-mail proposal to Mr. Nations and Ms. Keeley that included the team members' names and roles and a concise paragraph describing its intentions for its film, including

- The film's subject (e.g., a person, a group, an environment, a social issue).
- A brief plot synopsis.
- The plot conflict (e.g., man versus man, man versus nature, man versus society, social group versus social group).

The financial backers of the film (i.e., Mr. Nations and Ms. Keeley) either accepted or rejected the team's proposal, suggesting changes in the case of a rejection. After the production company modified its proposal, it resubmitted the proposal for approval.

Storyboard/screenplay script. Each team designed a storyboard using one of three free storyboard software programs that it selected after a collaborative review process. Some teams chose to develop their scripts online using Google Docs, while others used word-processing software. Before the teams started on their storyboards and scripts, the teachers reminded them of what to include and asked them to download the Storyboard and Script Rubric from the Film Festival wiki. The teachers evaluated each team's work according to the rubric's nine categories, which included

- Storyboard concept.
- Storyboard completeness.
- Storyboard clarity and neatness.
- Storyboard spelling and grammar.
- Script content.
- Script format.
- Script clarity.
- Use of time.
- Collaborative cooperation.

Some teams had their scriptwriters also write the screenplay, while other teams chose to work on the screenplay as a group. At the beginning of this stage, the teachers reminded students that a general script contains dialogue and actions, whereas a screenplay includes not only dialogue but also character actions and set and lighting descriptions. This stage was critical for students' success in the filming stage. When a team struggled, Mr. Nations and Ms. Keeley coached it through the thinking processes necessary to resolve its issues. On rare occasions, the teachers had to step in and make a strong suggestion so that the team could move forward and begin to film.

Filming. Before each team was approved to film specific scenes, the members needed to complete a pre–film production document that told Mr. Nations and Ms. Keeley where the team would be in the filming process, including their storyboard and on-set location, on a daily basis. When necessary, teams used a Movie Filming Schedule Form to sign up for time slots to film off campus. School staff members or school-approved volunteers provided adult supervision for off-campus filming before or after school or during class time. Although each team had two designated Flip-camera operators, the operators also needed to act in the film, so other team members had opportunities to film scenes as well. Each team worked collaboratively to ensure the use of proper lighting and camera angles.

Film editing/final production. There were times when each team worked as a whole and times when it broke apart into smaller groups of two to three students. For example, each team revised and edited its screenplay as a group, but when it came time to edit the film clips using iMovie, it often worked more smoothly to have only two or three team members involved in the process. A team's progress during the film editing/final production stage depended heavily on its dynamics and the director's ability to delegate. If a team could not resolve a dispute, Mr. Nations and Ms. Keeley were available to intervene. When a team believed its film was close to final-production quality, a peer team review took place. With facilitation by Mr. Nations or Ms. Keeley, another student team would view the film and complete a Team Evaluation Form with three rating scores: *very effective, somewhat effective,* and *little effect.* The evaluation form included 12 categories:

- Camera angles/shots.
- Camera movement.
- Lighting.
- Rule of thirds (thoughtful alignment of the subject within a grid of nine imaginary sections that act as a guide for framing the image; the subject or main point of interest should appear one-third or two-thirds of the way up or across the frame rather than in the center).
- Film opening (including text and music).
- Storyline and title.
- Character development.
- Costumes.
- Locations.

- Effective use of props.
- Editing (including transitions).
- Sound/music.

By the time the final film production was in the can, a subgroup within the team had most likely already embarked on the film poster stage.

Film poster. The Film Festival wiki listed links to film posters for teams to study, and teams could also conduct their own web research to locate posters. Team members examined and assessed the film posters according to a Movie Poster Rubric they were provided, which would be used to score their own film posters. The rubric included six categories:

- Film title.
- Names of main characters in poster footer.
- Images.
- Film tagline.
- Critic's testimonial for the film.
- Overall poster design.

Each team brainstormed and sketched its ideas by drawing freehand or using a graphic arts software program and created the final digital image in Adobe Photoshop. The final six full-color 11-inch-by-17-inch film posters were displayed in Ms. Keeley's classroom. The students posted black-and-white versions of the posters around the middle school and in local stores and restaurants with an announcement for the upcoming 8th Grade Film Festival.

Film festival. Two weeks prior to the film festival, which would be held in the high school auditorium, the teachers sent paper and digital film festival announcements to parents, guardians, and community members. On the evening of the culminating experience, the full-color film posters were displayed outside the auditorium doors, just as they would be at a movie theater. Because the students' summative assessment had already taken place, the evening focused on celebrating the students' diligence and dedication in creating their film productions. To generate an Academy Awards feel, film viewers were asked to vote the Best Actor, Best Actress, Best Picture, and Best Movie Poster. Ballot boxes were set up outside the auditorium so that attendees could vote as they enjoyed popcorn and soda at the end of the festival. The four film festival awards were announced and distributed during the 8th grade graduation ceremony and posted on the school's website.

A school board member who had attended the film festival asked Mr. Nations and Ms. Keeley to present one of the movies at the next board meeting. The middle school principal, Mr. Rogers, presented the movie that had won the Best Picture award and expressed his pride in Mr. Nations and Ms. Keeley for their effort to provide a modern-learning environment for students. He displayed a list of 21st century skills and spoke about how the screenplay-writing and film production unit had addressed each of them, enabling students to own their learning, make collaborative choices, and perform an authentic task.

Reactions and Reflections

Before the summer break began, Mr. Nations and Ms. Keeley met to debrief with Mrs. Jodi at the district office. Mrs. Jodi had attended the film festival and thought it had been a wonderful experience for all attendees. She also mentioned that the board members were impressed by what they had learned about the unit at the last meeting. In addition, her daughter, who would be in 8th grade the following school year, had asked her recently if she would be able to participate in the unit, too. Mr. Nations responded that he and Ms. Keeley were planning to teach the unit next year and that their two 8th grade colleagues wanted to collaborate as well.

Mrs. Jodi asked the two teachers to share what they had found to be most successful about the upgraded unit of study. Ms. Keeley shared that they had both been pleasantly surprised by students' enthusiasm and high level of engagement throughout the unit. Mr. Nations noted that they had received e-mails, cards, and in-person comments from parents and students who had found the unit to be a "big deal." He added that dividing the teaching and facilitating responsibilities equally between Ms. Keeley and him had been critical. Ms. Keeley observed that even though the students had been in two different classrooms each day, the two teachers had managed to deliver instruction and expectations seamlessly throughout the seven weeks.

Mr. Nations emphasized that the selection of a director for each team had proven to be a vital part of the process. Ms. Keeley agreed, noting that the director had been responsible for getting everything approved on the team's behalf. When a team needed a step or stage to be reviewed, the director met alone with one or both of the teachers. This arrangement saved the teachers from being surrounded by six students at one time and enabled them to clarify expectations with just the director, who in turn relayed the information to his or her team—a system that truly promoted student leadership and responsibility.

Mrs. Jodi then asked if the teachers had thought about what they might do differently next year. Mr. Nations said they had decided to concentrate on improving students' abilities to compose lifelike dialogue that fit their specific characters. Ms. Keeley added that she wanted the students to analyze more deeply how the selected film scenes they watched expressed mood. Both teachers mentioned creating the new role of assistant director to better balance the decision making. Mr. Nations mentioned that they had recently videoconferenced with a film professor at a local university who had expressed his willingness to visit their classrooms or videoconference with the students next year.

Mrs. Jodi was delighted with the success of the unit and looked forward to personally being a part of it the following year through her daughter's participation. She concluded the meeting by informing the teachers that she was currently writing a technology grant. Because Mr. Nations had mentioned that it would be an asset for the students to have better-quality cameras, if the district was awarded the grant she would contact him about what type they should purchase for the 8th graders to use next year.

On the last day of the school year, a teacher workday, Mr. Nations and Ms. Keeley met and recorded an information summary of what they had shared with Mrs. Jodi. They also added a few additional thoughts:

• **Higher-order thinking:** The majority of the unit required students to be critical thinkers. For example, students needed to use higher-order thinking to understand different possible interpretations of a character depending on the situation and point of view within a given scene.

• **Authentic performance/local connections:** Throughout the screenplay-writing and film production process, the students continually reminded one another that the local community would be watching the films. Having the film festival attendees vote for Best Actor, Best Actress, Best Picture, and Best Movie Poster added a dimension that, while frustrating for those who did not win, mirrored the real world of the Academy Awards.

• **Technology tools:** The students had learned some fundamentals in an introductory technology class. Some students had experience with iMovie, which all the teams used to make their films. We made certain that each team had at least one student comfortable using iMovie who took charge of film editing and demonstrated leadership throughout the process. In all, the students used Flip cameras, iPhones, an interactive whiteboard with a projector, and Mac computers and Apple software, including iMovie, GarageBand (used by some teams to create their own film music), Pages, and Keynote.

• **Web-based tools:** The Film Festival wiki proved worthwhile. The students used it often to perform tasks like leaving messages for one another in TodaysMeet.

Revisions

Over the summer, the four 8th grade teachers met for a day to discuss revisions to the screenplay-writing and film production unit of study, including

• The addition of job descriptions to the team roles to provide more clarity.

• The designation of three team members instead of two as scriptwriters.

• The revision of rubrics to provide greater specificity for each level on a 4–1 scale.

• A stronger emphasis on (and weekly evaluations of) personal and collaborative participation.

Mr. Nations announced that he had recently received an e-mail from Mrs. Jodi telling him that they had received the technology grant and would be getting new equipment, including handycams, tripods, and blank DVDs. He had also done some research and discovered Celtx, a web-based screenwriting and storyboarding tool that the classes could use next year. Using Celtx would enable students to develop their storyboards and scripts digitally and share them with their peers and teachers.

At the beginning of the following school year, the teachers were energized when they overheard the 8th graders chatting excitedly about participating in a film production "rite of passage" before going to high school.

Discussion Questions

1. Mr. Nations and Ms. Keeley needed an extensive length of time to upgrade the original unit of study. They believed their time investment was worthwhile because they were able to provide students with an authentic modern-learning

experience. What unit of study might you upgrade that would require a significant investment but result in a student-centered, 21st century performance task assessment and/or culminating experience?

2. The explanation for the CCR Capacity "Students demonstrate independence" states, "They build on others' ideas, articulate their own ideas, and confirm they have been understood. . . . More broadly, they become self-directed learners, effectively seeking out and using resources to assist them, including teachers, peers, and print and digital reference materials." Mr. Nations and Ms. Keeley conscientiously supported the students as independent learners and filmmakers. How might you embrace this particular capacity as you upgrade a unit of study?

3. Mrs. Jodi wrote a grant to purchase technology tools to enable the authentic incorporation of technology in instruction and assessment and enhance student ownership of learning. What obstacles in your school or district need to be addressed to ensure individual or small-group access to technology and web-based tools?

10

Social Justice Live!

Transformational Lenses		
Entry Points	**21st Century Clarifications**	**Technology Authenticity**
• Curriculum examinations • Instructional innovations	• Higher-order thinking • Collaborative environments • Local and global connections	• Web-based tools
Standards Connections		
English Language Arts College and Career Readiness Capacities • Students respond to the varying demands of audience, task, purpose, and discipline. • Students comprehend as well as critique. • Students value evidence. • Students use technology and digital media strategically and capably.		
Transformational Matrix Upgrade Zone: Transform		

Mr. Schultz was wrestling with an English language arts (ELA) unit of study that had become problematic. He wanted to move beyond the traditional social justice research project that his 8th grade class had done for the last several years. The unit had become a mundane writing project that required students to conduct research using outdated print resources available in the school library. He knew he wanted to create a transformation that would be motivating and engaging and deepen his students' learning.

His district's recent revision of its Internet use policy started him thinking about a possible upgrade for this unit. Students now had full access to web-based resources and social networking sites. He believed these tools could aid his students in their research and on the unit's final writing assessment.

Appraisal and Brainstorming

Mr. Schultz contacted members of his digital learning networks (DLNs) through Twitter, Facebook, ooVoo, and e-mail to solicit ideas for upgrading the unit. Although he heard from a variety of educators, the innovations that most resonated with him were those shared by Mr. Cannon, a technology integration specialist and teacher in an adjacent state.

During their first videoconference, Mr. Schultz told Mr. Cannon that in addition to placing a more authentic focus on current social justice issues, he wanted to improve the way the unit addressed the CCSS for ELA requisite that 8th graders be able to write an argument containing a claim and a counterclaim. He had found that one of his classes in particular was struggling with writing arguments. Their newfound access to the Internet hadn't helped: instead of selecting quality evidence to support their arguments, they tended to use the top search results regardless of their credibility or reliability (or lack thereof).

Mr. Cannon challenged Mr. Schultz to try out his upgrade with this struggling class. He pointed out that finding an authentic audience with which to share the arguments could improve students' learning and suggested that students post their arguments on a blog and have readers comment on them. Mr. Schultz liked this proposal. He speculated that he and Mr. Cannon could spread the word of the blog posts through their DLNs and ask students in his other two 8th grade ELA classes to leave comments. The comments could help students pinpoint revisions they might need to make or affirm that they had accurately conveyed their intended messages.

Mr. Cannon suggested that Mr. Schultz also consider making instructional innovations to support the struggling students. For example, it has proven beneficial to have students write short pieces focusing on a specific aspect of a complex composition, such as the establishment of a claim. He also suggested that Mr. Schultz have his students come up with their own norms for conducting peer reviews. Mr. Cannon had found it a worthwhile practice in his own teaching because it gave him more time to help where he was most needed and provide more individualized assistance.

Mr. Schultz agreed that such innovations would be helpful and added that he planned to spend more time facilitating class discussions about selected written arguments. He would also have students analyze claim–counterclaim pieces of writing and model quality claim–counterclaim writing during Writer's Workshop.

Commitment and Communication

When Mr. Schultz and Mr. Cannon met for a second videoconference session, Mr. Schultz said he had been thinking about how they stayed connected through their DLNs. After discussing a few possible ways to create authentic local and global connections, they decided to have the students participate in a virtual pre-research experience. Mr. Schultz thought that having his students make local and global connections during the pre-research phase and then blog their final arguments would constitute a 21st century upgrade, but he wanted to make sure those virtual connections had a purpose.

Mr. Cannon asked if each student would be selecting his or her own social justice issue to research and write on. Mr. Schultz explained that although he would like to do so, his students had previously studied local issues and decided that it would be best to focus on those. He would have students rank four issues—cyberbullying, child abuse, discrimination, and immigration—according to their level of interest, and he would divide them into groups accordingly. He would administer a survey using Google Forms, part of Google for Educators, a free online suite his district was encouraging teachers and students to use. He thought he might have students use other features of the suite, too, including Google Docs for individual and collaborative note taking and Google Sites to host the blog posts. Although he would require each student to write his or her own final argument for the blog, he wanted students to work collaboratively in their interest groups during the research phase.

Mr. Schultz also wanted to make sure the research phase accorded with a modern-learning environment. The two teachers discussed a blog post titled "Upgrade Your KWL Chart to the 21st Century" (Rosenthal Tolisano, 2011b) that described three new components to the traditional KWL research chart (What do we **K**now? What do we **W**ant to know? What have we **L**earned?) to make it a KWHLAQ chart. Here is what the additional letters represent:

• **H: H**ow will we find the information to answer the question "What do we want to know?" Students need to learn how to access, evaluate, analyze, organize, curate, and remix information. This stage is an important new intermediary between **W** (What do we want to know?) and **L** (What have we learned?).

• **A:** What **A**ction will we take once we have learned what we set out to learn? There was a time when information was set in stone; it wasn't easy to add personal perspectives or new information to the existing information. Nowadays, an abundance of tools enables us to collaborate with a worldwide audience and make continual revisions to our knowledge base. It is essential to make students aware of their power and the opportunities they have to take action.

• **Q:** What new **Q**uestions do we have? In *Curriculum 21* (Jacobs, 2010), Bill Sheskey observes that 21st century teaching is no longer about delivering answers but about instilling in students the ability to ask questions, and to continue asking new questions. Why would we want the research process to end with "What have we learned?" when we could leave it open-ended by asking, "What new questions do we have?"

Mr. Schultz noted that the **H** was crucial for helping students prepare for and engage in the research phase. In addition, providing students with an opportunity to connect with a local or global audience in real time would add to their current knowledge (**K**) and to their inquiries into what they wanted to know (**W**). He thought that making this type of authentic connection would also lead students to become more conscientious in their selection of credible and reliable sources.

Mr. Cannon asked Mr. Schultz to describe how he pictured the pre-research experience happening. Mr. Schultz said he envisioned students using LiveBinders as a virtual collection and curation tool. He would create interactive forums embedded in the binder using two web-based interactive tools: TodaysMeet, a closed chat service, and Wallwisher, a note-posting board. He could also embed collaborative Google Docs as a place for students to collect potential resources and useful websites.

Mr. Cannon suggested that Mr. Schultz add a tab that would link to the students' eventual blog posts. He also observed that to create a truly vital and interactive experience, it would be worthwhile to live stream the pre-research event.

Mr. Schultz shared his videoconferencing screen so that Mr. Cannon could help him create the LiveBinder. He started by creating the binder shell and four tabs, one for each of the social justice issues. Within each issue tab, he created three subtabs: one with an embedded TodaysMeet link, one with a Wallwisher link, and one with a Google Docs link. He then added four more tabs: one for uStream, the live interactive broadcast platform they would use; one for the student blog posts; one linking to his teacher website; and the last one linking to his professional blog. Finally, the two teachers brainstormed to come up with a name that would capture the purpose of the pre-research event. They eventually agreed on *Social Justice Live!*

During the next few weeks, Mr. Schultz prepared for the *Social Justice Live!* event, obtaining samples of high-quality argumentative writing to use during mini-lessons, independent work, and individual conferencing in Reader's Workshop and Writer's Workshop.

When it was time to introduce the social justice unit to his students, Mr. Schultz posed the provocative question, "Do our voices matter?" He then presented an overview of the unit:

> I've been working collaboratively with a colleague in another state who will be coming to our classroom for a special pre-research event. In a few days, I'm going to have each of you take an online survey to let me know which of four social justice issues you are most interested in researching. You'll be working in collaborative groups to research your selected issue. For the unit's final writing assessment, each of you will write your own argument based on the issue and post it on a blog.

During the first week and a half of the unit, Mr. Schultz's class spent Reader's Workshop focusing on arguments that contained quality claims and counterclaims. The arguments all related to social justice issues. Some were in blog format, which helped students grasp the concept of embedded links and the reader comment system. During Writer's Workshop, the students dissected authors' arguments, addressing the components of a quality argument with a writer's eye.

Early in the second week of the unit, Mr. Schultz displayed a KWHLAQ chart on an interactive whiteboard and explained its purpose and use. Next, he went online to the *Social Justice Live!* LiveBinder and explained that the students would be using this tool to collect information during the pre-research live event and to curate information during the research phase. He demonstrated how to interact with the binder and its embedded web-based tools and encouraged students to try out the interactive tools before the live event, which would take place on the following Monday.

In the middle of the second week, Mr. Schultz and Mr. Cannon sent messages through their DLNs announcing the *Social Justice Live!* event. Teachers in their state, North Carolina, as well as in Michigan, Texas, Washington, and Oregon, indicated that they would have their students participate and promised to retweet or forward the event announcement to others. Mr. Schultz asked Mr. Cannon to review the *Social Justice Live!* binder during the weekend preceding the event to make sure all the embedded web-based tools were working properly.

When Mr. Schultz and Mr. Cannon arrived at school on Monday, a teacher who was free during the event's class period asked if she could join in and assist the students. At the beginning of the period, Mr. Schultz displayed the *Social Justice Live!* binder on the interactive whiteboard and quickly reviewed the web-based tools within the binder. He asked the students to spend time within their selected issue tabs but also to explore the interactions within the other issue tabs during the live event.

Mr. Cannon reminded the students that event participants in other locations would be interacting with the class through postings, comments, and conversations in TodaysMeet or Wallwisher. He also called attention to the embedded Google Doc within each issue tab, where students could collect resources and web links to use during the research phase and, potentially, to support their final arguments. While he talked, Mr. Cannon walked around the room to make sure all the students had pulled up the *Social Justice Live!* binder on their laptops and were prepared to interact with one another and the outside participants during the live event. He reminded students that the participants would provide a range of information based on their own experiences—some of it solid evidence-based information, some of it opinion-based misinformation—and that the students would need to evaluate and analyze all the information they collected after the event to determine whether it was worthy of investigation and potential curation.

Mr. Schultz reminded students of their school's acceptable use policy, which permitted students' images and work to be filmed and posted online. Because the event would be streamed live on the Internet, anyone who preferred not to be filmed should sit outside the camera's range.

Just moments before the start of the 45-minute live event, Mr. Schultz and Mr. Cannon sent out one final announcement to their Twitter and Facebook followers. Then they turned on the uStream live feed, and *Social Justice Live!* officially began. The "social stream"—that is, the live stream plus the personal interactions among the students and event participants—started slowly. For the first five minutes, not much interaction took place either in the classroom or in the cloud. Then comments and questions began to trickle in. A teacher attending a technology conference in the Pacific Northwest who had seen the most recent tweet asked teachers at her table to participate during their break. These initial exchanges and an increase in event traffic ignited students' enthusiasm. They began to come up to the webcam and pose questions connected to their chosen issues. For example, when one student asked, "Are foster homes really as safe as they're supposed to be?" a variety of responses immediately came into the uStream chat box as well as the TodaysMeet conversation within the child abuse issue tab.

The discussions among students and participants continued at a steady pace. Time went by quickly, and it seemed as though the live event had just begun when Mr. Schultz announced that it was coming to a close. He thanked everyone who had participated and turned off the live video stream. Before he dismissed the class, he asked students to carefully review the conversations and information they had collected in the *Social Justice Live!* tabs before they met the following day, keeping in mind what they had learned about sources' credibility and reliability.

During the remainder of the week, students collaboratively researched their selected social justice issues and wrote rough drafts of their arguments based on the districtwide persuasive writing rubric. During Writer's Workshop, Mr. Schultz used several students' drafts to discuss establishing a claim and a counterclaim and citing credible and reliable sources. He also modeled posting a blog entry on his website to show students how to embed a hyperlink—a requirement for their blog posts. While the students collaboratively conducted peer revisions, Mr. Schultz facilitated as needed.

For two days after the live event, the students worked independently to finalize their arguments and post them on their individual student blogs in a wiki created by Mr. Schultz. When all the students had posted their blog entries, Mr. Schultz and Mr. Cannon sent out an announcement through their DLNs. By the time the students returned to class the next day, the blog posts had received comments. The students read the comments and, if they wished, used the feedback to help them revise their posts. After this final revision phase, each student received a final grade determined by Mr. Schultz and the student's peers, who used the rubric they had received after the *Social Justice Live!* pre-research event. Mr. Schultz's assessment and the peers' assessment were weighted equally.

Reactions and Reflections

Although the preparation for the upgrade ended up being more time-consuming than Mr. Schultz had imagined it would be, he told Mr. Cannon during a debriefing videoconference that he thought it had been a worthwhile investment. Students had actively collaborated with their peers; demonstrated increased conscientiousness in collecting, analyzing, and curating their research findings; learned to write an argument with a clear claim and counterclaim; and engaged in thoughtful peer revision of their drafts and analysis of the comments on their blog posts.

Mr. Schultz noted that his English language learners' writing in particular had shown significant improvement. He was not sure specifically what to attribute this growth to because he had made several instructional innovations, including scaffolding students' writing by having them write shorter, more tightly focused pieces; allowing more time for individualized feedback; and cultivating a higher level of student engagement during both the pre-research event and the subsequent research phase.

Mr. Cannon said that he had enjoyed reading the blog posts and was especially impressed considering the fact that Mr. Schultz had taught the upgraded unit to the class that struggled most with argumentative writing.

During the debriefing, Mr. Schultz captured their reflections in a collaborative Google Doc:

> • **Higher-order thinking:** The demands on students' cognition were high throughout the project. Students were continually asked to make informed decisions—for example, when they analyzed and curated the information they had collected and when they determined whether they had adequate evidence to support an argument's claim and counterclaim. They determined whether a source was credible and reliable by assessing the author's background and affiliations, examining multiple sources for corroboration, and taking into consideration an online source's URL extension (e.g., .edu versus .com). Requiring students to state why they believed a source was credible and relevant and to present those statements to their peers led them to think deeply about what they knew about the social justice issue.

The students demonstrated more thought and care than they had during previous writing experiences, when they blindly selected the first sources they found in the library's catalog or through an Internet key-word search. Reading and commenting on their peers' blog posts and evaluating comments left on their own posts also required critical thinking.

• **Collaboration and communication:** Students interacted meaningfully with one other during the pre-research, research, curation, and writing phases. They also worked collaboratively with outside participants during the *Social Justice Live!* experience.

• **Local and global connections:** Students interacted with other students and adults in their own state and in other U.S. states. Based on what we observed during the live event, the interactions were meaningful and authentic. Much of the information students collected came from people who had personal connections to the issues, which aided the students in their KWH work. The live feed enabled students to interact directly with their diverse audience. Comments and questions that came in through the uStream chat feature and through TodaysMeet and Wallwisher created a high level of engagement: students worked diligently in real time to answer questions, ask for clarification, and share their current thoughts and beliefs. At one point, there were more than 40 outside participants engaging in *Social Justice Live!*

• **Web-based tools:** The interactive broadcast platform uStream made a positive impact on the level of student participation during the live event. During the event, students communicated with one another and the outside participants using the web-based tools embedded in the LiveBinder. Guest participants interacting with the students through these tools further engaged students, and the tools provided students with 24/7 access to their collected (and eventually curated) information. The best part was when the students began informating and curating pertinent websites on their own, which they added appropriately within the LiveBinder.

• **Technology tools:** Students used available technology—including laptop computers, desktop computers, a web camera, and an interactive whiteboard—to interact with one another and to make local and global connections.

Mr. Schultz concluded the reflection document by stating his desire to further spiral this unit's transformation. Although students had commented on how much they enjoyed the entire process and felt that their voices had truly been heard, he thought there was room for improvement. He wanted to deepen the writing process by having the stronger writers in the class nurture their struggling peers. Also, intrigued by the high level of communication and collaboration afforded by web-based tools, he wanted to find ways to leverage his students' fascination with these tools to provide a more interactive critical analysis process of student writing for deeper articulation of peer responses during Writer's Workshop. He was not yet certain what that would look like, but he was looking forward to exploring the potential upgrade with Mr. Cannon and colleagues in his DLNs.

Revisions

As his school district began to integrate more curriculum expectations and professional development to align student learning to the CCSS for ELA, Mr. Schultz learned about various strategies, such as close readings, that would enable him to focus strategically on helping students choose words purposefully when writing arguments.

Mr. Schultz decided to expand the social justice argument-writing unit to his other ELA class periods the following year. He also planned to use the unit model for one or two of his 8th grade social studies units as a way of incorporating the CCSS for Literacy in History/Social Studies, Science, and Technical Subjects.

Mr. Cannon and Mr. Schultz kept in close contact throughout the remainder of the school year and the summer to share the latest websites and web-based applications that could enhance the live pre-research events, help students curate information during the research phase, and post their blog entries.

Discussion Questions

1. This snapshot provided a more detailed description of the two teachers' exchange of ideas and decision making during the commitment and communication stage than previous snapshots have. This was intentional; we wanted to convey the importance of continually brainstorming and refining decisions in planning a *transform* upgrade. Mr. Schultz reflected that preparing for the upgrade had taken more time than he had thought it would, but he knew it had all been worthwhile when he observed his students' increased engagement and the improvement in the quality of their writing. How do you think the amount of time spent planning and

implementing a *transform* upgrade might affect a teacher in the role of architect? In the role of contractor?

2. Mr. Schultz had not updated his research-based writing unit in several years, which was one reason he felt it was due for an upgrade. As you reflect on your instructional practice, can you think of any units that immediately jump out as being outdated? If so, how might you upgrade the units to more authentically reflect the 21st century environments your students will be entering after graduation?

3. This upgrade incorporated multiple web-based tools that were familiar to both teachers. Whom do you know whose orbit of ability includes knowledge of web-based tools and who could assist you in brainstorming and collaborating on potential transformations? If you do not know anyone who has this expertise, how might you find someone to assist you?

11

Science in the Cloud

Transformational Lenses		
Entry Points	**21st Century Clarifications**	**Technology Authenticity**
• Instructional innovations	• Collaborative environments	• Web-based tools
Standards Connections		
English Language Arts College and Career Readiness Capacities • Students build strong content knowledge. • Students use technology and digital media strategically and capably.		
Transformational Matrix Upgrade Zone: Outform		

Cloud computing refers to the use of hardware and software that are delivered as a service over a network—typically the Internet—rather than a hard drive or device-specific location. Instead of being stored on a computer or flash drive, documents are stored in the "cloud" and can be accessed privately or shared with others. Cloud computing enables multiple users to gain seamless access to shared documents, images, presentations, and other files, regardless of the hardware device (e.g., a desktop or laptop computer, a tablet, or a phone) each person uses. In addition to providing convenience, cloud storage and delivery capabilities are often free or minimally priced.

During a full-day curriculum work session, a district's high school science teachers met to align curriculum and instruction to new standards, address assessment revisions that needed to be made, and explore how continued budget cuts would affect their access to educational materials and resources.

Appraisal and Brainstorming

The district's budget had steadily declined to the point that schools hadn't been able to purchase new textbooks in more than seven years. Teachers had resorted to creating photocopied handouts of relevant information. Now the photocopier budget had been cut, and teachers would have to cut down on the number of copies they made. The conversation turned to possible solutions.

One of the teachers said, "I know some teachers who are starting to gather and store documents online, like you would on a flash drive. Does anyone know about this kind of service and whether or not it's something we might consider using with our students?"

The workshop facilitator mentioned several cloud services, including Dropbox (www.dropbox.com), Box (www.box.com), and Google Docs, as well as those offered by Amazon and iTunes. He and a few of the teachers who were familiar with the services took the other workshop participants on a quick online tour. After a brief discussion of the various services' capabilities, the teachers brainstormed questions that would help them decide which cloud service would be the best fit for their district:

- What is the cost of each service?
- Which services may be blocked by our district's filtering system?
- What would the teacher learning curve be for each service?
- Do any of the services require use of a particular hardware device?

- Is there an issue of free or paid student access for each service?
- What do we need to consider regarding equity of access for students, some of whom do not have Internet access at home?
- Will students be able to easily access documents and media files? Will students be able to turn in assignments and projects through the service individually and collaboratively?
- Will students be able to share resources and work collaboratively in the service?

The teachers decided to break into teams of three to come up with answers to their posed questions. After about an hour of exploration, including making phone calls to some of the services, they came back together to share what they had discovered.

Their research eliminated Google Docs, which they agreed would be the most convenient but was blocked by their district's filtering system. The Amazon and iTunes services needed to connect to specific devices. Although they found appropriate apps available across devices, the teachers felt that there were too many variables to use either of these two services. Dropbox and Box were the finalists: both met the criteria for accessibility and would allow students to work individually and collaboratively.

During the last part of the workshop, the participants appraised their remaining units of study for the school year and thought about how best to utilize the cloud services to compensate for their budget constraints and provide students with access to current information.

Commitment and Communication

At their high school's next science department meeting, two of the workshop participants—Mr. Williams and Ms. Prince—shared that they had been using Dropbox to sync and share files across their work computers, home computers, and digital devices. After the science teachers briefly discussed the decisions made at the districtwide workshop, they determined that the entire science department would use the free version of Dropbox as its cloud service. Mr. Williams and Ms. Prince would be the go-to people for questions and support.

After each teacher in the department created his or her own Dropbox account, Mr. Williams and Ms. Prince gave a fuller explanation of the service. They explained that teachers could use it to collect materials and resources with their students, and students could use it to turn in work electronically. One teacher commented that this last feature alone made it worth using: some of the teachers in the department had been having students turn in their work via e-mail, but it was a cumbersome process.

The teachers agreed that at their next department meeting they would begin to assemble materials and resources needed for the upcoming grading period's units of study. These materials would include handouts in Microsoft Word, PowerPoint presentations, videos, lab manuals, and assignments.

A few teachers who had limited experience using cloud services voiced their discomfort. The department decided to divide into teams of two so that teachers who were less at ease using web-based tools would have more-experienced partners to support them.

At the beginning of the next department meeting, one team used an interactive whiteboard to project its Dropbox account while the remaining teams opened their accounts on their laptops. They decided to begin creating Dropbox folders for each general science course before moving on to the advanced placement and specialized courses. For each course, each class would have its own folder, and each student would have a folder within that class folder. The class folders would be accessible only to the teacher and the class members, and student folders would be accessible only to the individual student and the teacher.

To access the folders, students would need to create individual Dropbox accounts, for which an e-mail address was required. Most students already had e-mail addresses, and it would be a simple matter to help those who didn't to create e-mail accounts.

Ms. Prince explained that Dropbox would give teachers and their students full access to materials and resources regardless of their location or the device they were using. This led to the question of whether all students had equal access to the Internet—an important issue, since they would be using this web-based tool for critical learning and assessments. After some discussion, the teachers concluded that most students had Internet access at home, but that they would make sure all students were able to get sufficient Internet access at school and at local libraries. They also decided to give students the option of receiving printed copies of the materials and turning in their assignments and assessments the traditional way.

Some teachers were concerned that relying on a cloud-based service could leave them vulnerable to unexpectedly losing all their files. Mr. Williams explained that when a user initially downloaded the software, Dropbox installed a web-linked folder on the device's hard drive. Therefore, even if this web-based tool suddenly disappeared, all of the uploaded files and materials would be saved.

In subsequent meetings, the science department members continued to share their experiences using the cloud process in their classrooms. Mrs. Doran shared that she had experienced some frustration with the time it took to set up individual student accounts and the challenge of managing who had access to which folders. Ms. Prince explained that the frustration was a natural part of getting used to the new web-based tool. In addition, the fact that they had made the upgrade later in the school year meant that they hadn't gotten as much time to get used to it as they would have had they started at the beginning of the school year. Another teacher expressed confidence that next year the initial setup process would be much easier.

During a meeting several weeks later, the teachers excitedly discussed the benefits of using the cloud service to manage resources. Mr. Matthews noted that dropping a document in Dropbox for his students to use was so much easier and less time-consuming than passing it out in class. Others agreed that they were saving a considerable amount of time by not making copies. Many teachers had all but stopped using the photocopier.

By the end of the school year, students were adept at the new Dropbox procedures of accessing files and turning in work. They appreciated that unlike the district's computer network, to which they had access only while at school, Dropbox allowed them access anywhere, any time, and on any device.

Reactions and Reflections

During the last department meeting of the school year, the teachers reflected on their Science in the Cloud upgrade. They revisited the conversations they had had at the districtwide workshop and found that their situation had improved. They no longer felt frustrated by their lack of up-to-date textbooks. They had found that uploading current materials and audiovisual resources into Dropbox made for authentic learning and engaged students. Cloud storage also enabled them to provide students with opportunities to read and respond to complex texts based on the courses' content-knowledge expectations. One teacher commented that he liked that he and his students were able to access and share materials and interact in a protected and private manner anytime they liked. Traditional excuses for not being able to turn in an assignment or for forgetting a textbook or handout became irrelevant.

On an interactive whiteboard, Ms. Prince created a new Dropbox folder titled "Our Reflections in Dropbox." She then minimized the screen and created a new Microsoft Word document to capture the teachers' reflections, which she would save and upload after their meeting. She recorded the following comments:

• **Collaboration:** Using cloud-based resources, students were able to receive texts and materials from their teachers as well as upload their own files. There was a high degree of collaboration among the teachers as they learned how to make the best use of the web-based tool. Some students got the opportunity to create digital bookshelves—collections of relevant resources for projects and performance tasks shared by cooperative groups.

• **Technology tools:** An important aspect to the cloud-based resource sharing was that each student was able to access all the materials and resources, regardless of the device he or she used.

• **Web-based tools:** Students and teachers found using Dropbox to access and share resources a welcome alternative to traditional handouts. Students were able to print out the materials if they preferred.

• **Information literacy:** Ms. Prince was initially concerned by some students' use of Dropbox to share music and movies, but she used their actions as an opportunity to discuss appropriate use of the Internet and web-based services, particularly at school or on the job. She extended the discussion to the issues of "borrowing" content without attribution and the use of proper citations. She told her class about Creative Commons, a nonprofit organization that enables online content creators to protect copyright while allowing certain uses of their work. She explained that different types of licenses gave permission for different levels of use (e.g., permission to share content with attribution or to remix content with attribution to the original content creator).

• **Evidence-based opportunities:** Students had access to multiple types of texts that gave them opportunities to practice comparative analysis, evidence-based questioning and reasoning, and writing from sources for information or argument. All of these tasks were aligned to the CCSS for ELA and Literacy in History/Social Studies, Science, and Technical Subjects for grades 6–12.

As the meeting drew to a close, the teachers agreed that they were pleased with the implementation. They acknowledged, however, that although they had transformed their traditional mode of managing materials and resources, they needed to explore further how to use cloud computing to improve student learning.

Revisions

During the summer, most of the teachers in the science department stayed connected. One of the teachers shared that he had added the Dropbox app to his new iPad, along with a companion app that would enable him to make notations on digitally submitted student work and then drop the annotated work back into the shared folders.

During the first department meeting of the new school year, Mr. Williams shared an idea based on the ELA CCR Capacity of students being able to use technology and digital media strategically and capably. He suggested that this year, each course should provide authentic opportunities for students to create their own shared folders, annotate one another's work, and choose how to organize their folders by topic and theme. Even the teachers who had initially been wary about using web-based tools expressed enthusiasm about this instructional innovation.

Ms. Prince and Mr. Williams also mentioned that they wanted to build in some time during an upcoming department meeting to explore other types of web-based tools they planned to use this year and invited their colleagues to join them. They were especially excited at the prospect of incorporating a social bookmarking service, which would enable students to curate relevant websites when conducting research.

Discussion Questions

1. The upgrade zone for this snapshot is *outform*. Some might perceive the snapshot as simply automating an instructional practice. How could this transformation be spiraled into an informating or amplifying upgrade?

2. In contrast to most of the other upgrades described in this book, Science in the Cloud addresses three transformational lenses. Looking back at the descriptions of entry points, 21st century clarifications (including technology authenticity), and standards connections in Chapter 2, what are some additional transformational lenses you might suggest for this upgrade?

3. Given the current economic climate, what insights from this snapshot might help you use web-based tools to support learning and teaching in your own school or district?

12

Pinterest Art Critiques

Transformational Lenses		
Entry Points	**21st Century Clarifications**	**Technology Authenticity**
• Performance task assessments • Curriculum examinations • Instructional innovations	• Collaborative environments • Local connections	• Technology tools • Web-based tools
Standards Connections		
English Language Arts College and Career Readiness Capacities • Students respond to the varying demands of audience, task, purpose, and discipline. • Students comprehend as well as critique. • Students value evidence. • Students use technology and digital media strategically and capably.		
Transformational Matrix Upgrade Zone: Transform		

A high school's three art teachers are involved in a multidistrict consortium of art educators that meets quarterly, focusing on common topics, themes, and instructional practices based on state standards. During a meeting near the beginning of the school year, the teachers discussed the implications of the Common Core State Standards for Literacy in History/Social Studies, Science, and Technical Subjects for grades 6–12—specifically, the writing standards (WHST). Although some of the high schools in the consortium had incorporated reading and writing across disciplines, others had not. Even in the art classes that did integrate writing, students were often writing explanatory or narrative critiques. The first WHST standard requires students to write arguments containing evidence-based claims and counterclaims. One teacher, whose students tended to write informal art critiques based on personal opinion, commented that this expectation took art critique to a new level.

Appraisal and Brainstorming

As the three art teachers carpooled back to their school, Mrs. Sheldon suggested that they have their students write argumentatively for an art critique coming up in the general Art II course they all taught. Mr. Maidens responded that they would need to begin by exploring what writing an argument truly entails. Mrs. Gorman suggested that they consult with one of the English teachers at the high school.

Accordingly, they met with Mr. Coughlin and shared with him their goal to have their art students write arguments for an upcoming performance task assessment (the art critique). They explained that they needed to first learn about argumentative writing themselves. As Mr. Coughlin began his explanation, Ms. Bigelow, another English teacher, walked in and joined the conversation. She suggested that because of the learning curve involved, the art teachers might want to take a small first step by having their students write just a claim rather than a full argument with a claim and a counterclaim.

Mr. Coughlin showed Ms. Bigelow the examples of student critiques that Mrs. Sheldon, Mr. Maidens, and Mrs. Gorman had brought. They were written informally, in the first person, and based heavily on personal opinion.

Ms. Bigelow recalled from her own experience taking an art course in college a few years ago that art critique includes four major areas: *description, analysis, interpretation,* and *judgment.* She remembered that in her critiques she was required to

- Describe the work and, if appropriate, the artist.
- Analyze the organization of the composition.
- Describe the aesthetic effect of the work on herself as a viewer.
- Provide her personal interpretation of the artwork's success or failure at achieving its apparent goal.

She observed that having the high school art students include all four areas in their critiques while writing in a formal style and maintaining a third-person point of view would likely be a challenge for them. Mr. Coughlin suggested that the teachers make learning to write using a formal style the main focus for this project.

Mrs. Sheldon asked how the art critiques they had brought would read if students had written them as arguments. Mr. Coughlin and Ms. Bigelow scanned through the student critiques and selected one to rewrite as an example for the art teachers. They chose a critique that was attached to a colored-pencil sketch of what appeared to be people exiting a slightly abstract grove of trees. Mr. Coughlin and Ms. Bigelow worked collaboratively for a few moments and wrote a revision of the critique as an argument (see Figure 12.1).

FIGURE

12.1 Two Art Critiques

Original Critique (Opinion)

Your sketch of a grove of trees used a variety of pencil colors. The variations of thin lines and thick lines added contrast in the grove. The color choice used around the people leaving the forest is interesting because it appears to make them appear to be fleeing. The only thing I cannot tell is what time of day it is supposed to be. Is the gold coloring the sunlight glistening or the leaves changing color? Being consistent with lighting direction can help convey a time frame. For example, if you want it to be morning, the side of the trees where the sun is coming up needs to be brighter and the opposite side of the trees needs to be shadowed.

Revised Critique (Argument)

In the sketch "Grove on the Move" by Andrea, shades of brown and white highlight the trunks and lower branches of the trees on the right side of the path. This technique produces an effect of parallel light as the sun, low in the sky, illuminates the trees. This effect is further enhanced by the use of a shadowy background and lighter foreground. As the figures in the foreground run toward the viewer, Andrea successfully creates a sense of hope as they escape the darkness and emerge into the light.

Mr. Coughlin explained how the revised critique was written as a formal argument and addressed the four areas of art critique:

Description: In the sketch "Grove on the Move" by Andrea, shades of brown and white highlight the trunks and lower branches of the trees on the right side of the path.

Analysis: This technique produces an effect of parallel light as the sun, low in the sky, illuminates the trees. This effect is further enhanced by the use of a shadowy background and lighter foreground.

Interpretation: As the figures in the foreground run toward the viewer, Andrea successfully (**Judgment**) creates a sense of hope as they escape the darkness and emerge into the light.

The art teachers were intrigued by the distinction between the original and the revised critique. Ms. Bigelow reminded them that unlike critiques written in English class, their students' critiques would be using aspects of the artwork as evidence rather than textual evidence, so their claims needed to be based on the works' visual message or intent.

Commitment and Communication

The art teachers thanked Mr. Coughlin and Ms. Bigelow for their assistance and asked if they would be willing to continue supporting them as they worked on upgrading the performance task assessment. Both English teachers said they would be happy to assist and offered to help the art teachers develop a rubric focused on the requisites of writing a formal critique.

During a faculty meeting the following week, Mr. Root, the principal, reminded the teachers that part of the district's "Next Generation" short- and long-range plan required each school to provide evidence that teachers were meaningfully and authentically integrating technology and web-based tools into classroom instruction and assessment. As he had done throughout the school year, Mr. Root turned the floor over to the faculty for a technology showcase—a 10-minute period in which any teacher could share software or web-based tools and applications that he or she had found beneficial.

One of the social studies teachers, Mrs. Dzielak, used the meeting room's computer and a whiteboard to share an interactive online site called Pinterest. Mrs. Dzielak told the faculty to think of Pinterest as a virtual pinboard featuring topic- or theme-based images curated by users. She explained that because Pinterest is also a social networking site, users can visit others' pinboards, repin images to their own pinboards, and "like" images, as in Facebook. Pinterest's mission statement explains that the goal of the website is to "connect everyone in the world through the 'things' they find interesting." Mrs. Dzielak navigated through various pinboards and explained that she had been having her students create pinboards related to what they were learning and researching in their Global History and Geography course.

After the meeting, Mr. Maidens told Mrs. Sheldon and Mrs. Gorman that he had an idea for using Pinterest in their upcoming performance task assessment. Each student would

• Create a digital artwork based on predetermined criteria and geared toward a particular audience. This assignment would correspond with the ELA CCR Capacity of responding to the varying demands of audience, task, and purpose.

• Upload the finished artwork to the Pinterest pinboard created for the project.

• Select a peer's pinned artwork to critique.

• Study the selected artwork, draft his or her critique using an argument claim, and work with a peer (not the creator of the artwork being critiqued) to revise the argument using a rubric provided at the onset of the project.

• Log in to Pinterest to post his or her critique of the selected artwork.

• Review the critiques posted for his or her own artwork.

• Share his or her reflections about the overall quality of critiques during a class debriefing of the project.

Mr. Maidens added that because students would have full access to the uploaded artwork, they would be able to critique the artwork of peers who were not in their own class. Mrs. Sheldon and Mrs. Gorman liked this upgrade idea. They noted that the performance task assessment authentically incorporated students' artwork, standards-based writing criteria, and a web-based tool. Mrs. Sheldon commented that she thought students' greatest challenge might turn out to be not writing in a formal style but creating art for a specific audience. In the past, they had encouraged students to use art projects as an open channel for personal expression.

Before continuing the planning process, they met with Mr. Root to discuss potential parent concerns about making students' names, avatars, or images public on Pinterest. Mr. Root explained that the district had established a policy allowing teachers and students to access social networking websites to communicate, collaborate, and interact with people globally. Parents and guardians were informed of this policy when their children began attending school in the district. Still, he recommended that as a courtesy they might want to allow students to opt out of posting their art and writing comments in Pinterest. A student who opted out would still create an artwork and write a critique, but he or she would not upload any images or post comments. He also reminded the teachers to tell students not to use the school or district name when they created the pinboard for the project, as it would be a violation of Children's Internet Protection Act (CIPA) rules. Likewise, they must remind students to use only their first names and never mention the school or district name in their comments. Mr. Maidens said that he would make sure he gave the collaborative pinboard a generic name like "Our Art Board."

The art teachers decided to provide the students with three choices of digital artwork to create, each aimed at a different audience:

- A cover design for a book, magazine, or music album.
- An event announcement or invitation.
- A restaurant menu.

They worked collaboratively with Mr. Coughlin and Ms. Bigelow to develop a rubric with a four-point scale for the upcoming performance task assessment. They chose to include the criteria for both the digital artwork and the textual critique in one rubric with three categories, including

- **Artwork.** Criteria focus on appropriateness of artwork for intended audience, including use of text, images, layout, and colors and value.
- **Art critique.** Criteria focus on the major areas of art critique: description, analysis, interpretation, and judgment.
- **Comment.** Criteria focus on quality commenting that maintains consistent use of formal style, appropriate tone, and third-person point of view.

The art teachers and English teachers prepared three mini-lessons to reinforce what the students had been learning in their English courses about writing an argument. Each teacher introduced the week-and-a-half-long digital artwork unit to his or her class by displaying Pinterest on an interactive whiteboard and providing details about the project, both for the artwork and the critique.

Students were excited about the opportunity to work online. The district had recently added computers to the media center to provide students with increased accessibility, which greatly benefited students who did not have computers or Internet access at home. The art teachers had reserved computers in the media center to enable students to access Pinterest and write their critiques using their choice of word-processing software.

Throughout the first week of the unit, the teachers made sure that each student had established a Pinterest account, was comfortable using Pinterest, and was aware of the CIPA rule requiring him or her to use only a first name and not to post the school or district's name or image.

During the first two days of the unit, the students worked on their art projects using Adobe InDesign. On the third or fourth day, each of the three art teachers modeled the critique process to his or her class with one of the other teachers as a partner. For example, for one class, Mrs. Sheldon paired with Mr. Maidens. First, Mr. Maidens, modeling the role of the artist, displayed one of three examples of the allowable digital artwork projects to the class: the cover of a popular regional magazine, a birth announcement for a Spanish teacher's baby boy, or a menu from a popular local eatery. He explained that he had uploaded the image of his chosen artwork to the project pinboard in Pinterest. Mrs. Sheldon then told the class that she had chosen Mr. Maidens's artwork to critique. Mr. Maidens left the classroom to demonstrate that he would not take part in the critique. The students then made observations about the artwork and offered Mrs. Sheldon ideas to include in her critique based on the rubric's criteria.

Mrs. Sheldon then wrote her critique and reminded the students that after they drafted their own critiques, they would work with a peer to review and revise their drafts. When ready, each student would post his or her final critique to the appropriate pinned image.

When Mr. Maidens came back into the classroom, he read aloud and reflected on the critique of his work, noting how Mrs. Sheldon used evidence from his artwork to support her claim. He then explained that after all of the project participants had posted their critiques on Pinterest and had had an opportunity to reflect on the critiques of their own work, each class would hold a debriefing session to share their reactions to the critiques.

By Friday afternoon, the students had uploaded their digital artwork to the project pinboard, although a few students needed help from their peers to do so. On Monday, the students spent the entire class period selecting a peer's artwork and writing their personal critiques in the media center. Toward the end of the period, the teacher asked the students to print out their drafts to bring to class on Tuesday.

On Tuesday, the teacher and students reviewed the rubric and discussed the criteria for earning the maximum score in each of the rubric's categories. Students then formed pairs to work on revising their drafts. The teacher circulated among the review teams, facilitating discussion and answering questions that arose. At the end of the revision process, the teacher directed the students to post their critiques to the appropriate artwork image on the project pinboard by the end of the day.

When the students arrived to class on Wednesday, they excitedly discussed the critiques they had been reading—not only for their own class but also for the other two. During the first half of the class period, the teacher displayed the pinboard on the interactive whiteboard and led a discussion based on the critiques. Students took turns coming up to the whiteboard to select specific artwork, read the corresponding critiques, and share their reactions. During the second half of class, the students broke into smaller groups based on their chosen artwork and written critique to discuss the quality of their arguments. The teacher visited each small group and joined the conversations when appropriate. The class came together once again toward the end of the period to recap the process of writing a quality argument while maintaining a formal style.

During the debriefing sessions, students expressed that writing, posting, and reading the critiques had been a positive experience. Many observed that the formal style of the critiques had made them more open and willing to hear what the commentators were saying. A few students mentioned that when they had gone through art critiques in the past, they had felt that the comments were often subjective, and sometimes they had felt picked on.

Many of the students in all three classes asked if they would get the opportunity to write art critiques again that semester. After some discussion among themselves, the three teachers shared with their classes that they might be able to do another critique for the final unit of the semester, which involved oil painting. They explained that students would need to take photos of their artwork and scan the images into a computer before pinning them to the project pinboard. The students were enthusiastic, commenting that they were already looking forward to the oil painting unit.

Reactions and Reflections

The art teachers met with the English teachers the day after the unit's completion and shared their excitement about the project and its results. They noted that the unit had gone better than they had expected, and they were pleased with both the level of students' engagement and the quality of their writing. Mr. Coughlin and Ms. Bigelow shared that they had read the critiques on Pinterest and were impressed by the quality of many of the critiques. The teachers displayed the project pinboard on the interactive whiteboard and took some time to read and discuss some of the critiques together.

The art teachers recalled the conversation they had had with Mr. Root about the CIPA rules. Only two students had opted out of the web-based project, instead sharing their artwork and critiques in class. Both students wanted to participate fully in the critique for the oil painting unit, however, and asked the art teachers to talk to their parents.

The teachers recorded their reflections on the upgraded unit in a collaborative Google Doc:

- **Critical thinking and communication:** Students were expected to write formal critiques of their peers' work and provide objective, evidence-based reasoning for their thinking. In the past, the art critiques had been more subjective, based on opinion.
- **Local connections:** Using a web-based tool that made their images and comments public seemed to drive students to create higher-quality work. Knowing that their art and critiques could be seen not only by their classmates but also, potentially, by anyone around the world ended up being an unexpected motivator.
- **Analysis and evaluation:** It was interesting and exciting to watch the students in action during the revision process. They held one another accountable for including the required four areas of an art critique in their drafts and for writing their critiques in the third person and in a formal style. Providing the rubric at the onset of the unit helped students create high-quality artwork and critiques, and elicited thoughtful comments during the debriefing session.
- **Technology tools:** Most students accessed the Pinterest pinboard using school computers, and a few students chose to use their own digital devices.
- **Web-based tools:** The web-based tool Pinterest played an important role in the unit's success. When the students indicated that they wanted to do another critique, we knew we had hit a home run! Some students chose to write their critiques using a collaborative web-based tool like Google Docs and granted access to the peer reviewer so that both could work in the online document simultaneously.

- **Argumentative writing:** Before this upgrade, much of the writing in art class centered on opinion-based reflective pieces that did not require students to analyze artwork beyond aesthetics. Although the students didn't write multipage argumentative essays, their critiques did provide evidence that they were engaging in higher-order thinking and using evidence-based logic. The majority of the critiques evaluated how well the artworks achieved their intended message based on their audience, task, and purpose.

Although Mr. Coughlin and Ms. Bigelow shared the art teachers' enthusiasm over the success of the project, they reminded them of the WHST standard stating that high school students should be writing formal arguments containing both a claim and a counterclaim. Mrs. Gorman replied that they were planning to have students in their advanced art classes select and conduct research on an artist or a piece of artwork from a certain period. The research project would require them to write a full, formal argument using textual evidence from credible sources. The art teachers asked Mr. Coughlin and Ms. Bigelow if they would be willing to aid them in preparing the research project and creating an appropriate rubric. Both English teachers said they would be delighted to continue assisting the art teachers.

Toward the end of the meeting, the art teachers shared their excitement at the prospect of discussing their project at the next meeting of the art teachers' consortium. They planned to inform their colleagues that the English department had played a critical role in the success of the upgraded performance task assessment.

Revisions

During the summer, Mrs. Sheldon, Mr. Maidens, and Mrs. Gorman kept in contact and occasionally got together to discuss plans for the coming school year. During one of the meetings, their conversation turned to providing more opportunities for their students to take the project to a global level. Mr. Maidens had begun to think about how they could create an art-critique forum examining famous artwork using Google Art Project (www.googleartproject.com) or Museum Box (www.museumbox.e2bn.org) as well as social networking tools such as Pinterest or Flickr. Mrs. Sheldon had read about an online project that required students to visit a museum virtually and analyze a particular style of artwork. For example, students can browse the Guggenheim's permanent collection at www.guggenheim.org/new-york/collections/collection-online.

The teachers also outlined the research project for their advanced art classes and looked forward to continuing its development with Mr. Coughlin and Ms. Bigelow once the school year started.

Discussion Questions

1. The art teachers knew they needed assistance from the English teachers' orbits of ability to implement their upgrade. During the debriefing session, Mrs. Sheldon noted that the collaboration between the two departments had been crucial to the project and mentioned that they would not have seen the level of engagement or the quality of writing they did without the help of the English teachers. Does your school or district foster a climate where educators are comfortable with not knowing everything and with seeking out colleagues' orbits of ability, either in person or virtually? If so, how might this climate help you in upgrading units of study? If not, how might you and your colleagues help create a climate promoting collaborative learning and teaching?

2. During the planning stage, the art teachers went to their principal, Mr. Root, to discuss the use of the web-based social networking tool Pinterest. He reminded them that district policy permitted students to access social networking sites but that according to CIPA rules, the teachers were responsible for setting boundaries. Working within your own school or district's Internet use policies, how might you purposefully incorporate 21st century web-based tools and environments that many students already access outside school?

3. The ELA CCR Capacities are intentionally applicable to a variety of disciplines. The art teachers' desire to include argumentative writing in the Art II course is an example of how these capacities may be applied across the content areas. What might you do, and with whom would you work, to authentically and meaningfully incorporate the ELA CCR Capacities into the various disciplines at your school?

13

Common Core State Standards Professional Development

Transformational Lenses		
Entry Points	**21st Century Clarifications**	**Technology Authenticity**
• Instructional innovations	• Collaborative environments	• Web-based tools
Transformational Matrix Upgrade Zone: Outform		

Mrs. Jay, the elementary principal in a K–12 school, had formerly been the school's K–12 curriculum coordinator. Although her new title came with new priorities, she was still actively involved in curriculum design and instructional practice across all the grades. School administrators, teachers, and parents had recently decided to align the K–12 curriculum to the Common Core State Standards (CCSS). In addition, the school had been working on integrating technology and web-based tools in more meaningful and purposeful ways. Mrs. Jay thought it was important to develop her own professional expertise and model what an educator in a 21st century educational environment looked like. She felt strongly that if she was going to ask teachers to take risks, she needed to be willing to do so as well.

Appraisal and Brainstorming

At the beginning of the fourth quarter of the school year, Mrs. Jay met with Mr. Merritt, the superintendent, and Mr. Sorrell, the middle school principal, to outline a CCSS implementation plan. Most teachers at the school did not know much about the standards beyond what they had learned in a few faculty meetings led by Mrs. Jay and a mini-team of elementary and secondary teachers from the school, which had provided insight into the standards and their development.

The three administrators reflected on the school's recent completion of a two-year action-research pursuit using *The Art and Science of Teaching: A Comprehensive Framework for Effective Instruction* (Marzano, 2007). The teachers had enthusiastically received and implemented the book's strategies, and the administrators wanted to bridge that work to a new undertaking: revising the curriculum according to the Common Core. They knew that few teachers had explored the standards in depth or knew the full impact the standards would have on the curriculum. The administrators decided that the final inservice of the school year should cultivate a deeper understanding of the structures of the Common Core State Standards for English Language Arts and Literacy in History/Social Studies, Science, & Technical Subjects (CCSS for ELA) and the Common Core State Standards for Mathematics (CCSSM). Mrs. Jay volunteered to take on the responsibility of the inservice.

Commitment and Communication

Mrs. Jay had approximately three weeks to prepare for the CCSS inservice. Honoring her administrative colleagues' schedules, and not wanting the teachers on the CCSS mini-team to have to leave their classrooms at this time of year, she decided that she would complete much of the preparation solo. She asked to meet with the elementary-level members of the CCSS mini-team after school one day prior to the inservice to talk through the planned content and delivery and make any necessary revisions based on their input.

She wanted to begin her planning process by collecting data. She decided to conduct a survey to gauge what teachers already knew and what they needed to know. She had often used a free version of Survey Monkey, a web-based survey and analytical tool, with administrators, board members, and parents. She constructed a five-question survey and sent the link to the teachers via e-mail, asking them to complete the survey within three days.

Thirty-five of the 60 teachers in the school took the survey. Although she had hoped for 100 percent participation, she thought the results likely represented the faculty's understanding of the CCSS. Using Survey Monkey's analytic features, she discovered that the majority of teachers had not read or learned about the standards on their own. Some teachers voiced concern about how the inclusion of the CCSS would affect current schoolwide instructional practices, while others were excited at the prospect of using the CCSS to help them assess student learning. Several teachers commented that they appreciated her using the online tool to gather the data and said they would like to use Survey Monkey in their own classrooms. Although these comments were not a direct response to any of the survey questions, Mrs. Jay was pleased with the teachers' desire to use a web-based tool.

Mrs. Jay knew she needed to gain a better understanding of the CCSS for ELA and CCSSM. Realizing that this would take a significant amount of time, she consulted with Mr. Merritt and Mr. Sorrell and decided to focus the inservice specifically on the CCSS for ELA, which involved all the disciplines. She studied the original documents at the Common Core State Standards Initiative website (www.corestandards.org) as well as the version on her state's department of education website, since it would be helpful for the teachers to familiarize themselves with the additional information provided by the state website. Based on her notes on the CCSS documents (including the standards and the appendices), she conducted general keyword searches to locate additional information on how other states, institutions, and educators were implementing or preparing to implement the CCSS.

After about a week of exploration, Mrs. Jay began to feel overwhelmed by the sheer volume of information she had found on the Internet. She asked herself, *Where should we, as a K–12 faculty, begin the process of designing curriculum based on the CCSS for ELA?* Her biggest concern was that if she felt this overwhelmed now, the teachers might feel even more so during the inservice. She did not want to present the CCSS for ELA as just one more thing to incorporate into an already extensive long-range curriculum and instruction improvement plan.

Knowing she would have only 90 minutes to conduct the inservice, she kept returning to a desire to keep it simple, informative, and applicable to the summer planning the teachers would soon be doing. She shared her concerns informally with the elementary-level members of the CCSS mini-team. They agreed that less is often more.

Mrs. Jay decided to solicit advice from Ms. Searle, a friend and colleague who was a curriculum design specialist. She e-mailed Ms. Searle asking if she could consult her over the phone about her upcoming presentation. Ms. Searle suggested they videoconference instead so that they could view each other's screens and consult documents during the conversation. Ms. Searle had helped Mrs. Jay create a Skype account a few months earlier. Mrs. Jay commented that she was still not used to thinking "21st century" and needed to remember to use videoconferencing as a method of communication.

During the videoconference, Mrs. Jay took notes and listened intently to Ms. Searle's suggestions, which included using cloud-based services to find and curate information and make it easily accessible to the teachers. At the end of their conversation, as they turned to personal matters, Ms. Searle encouraged Mrs. Jay to watch a family celebration video on YouTube uploaded by Mr. Liam, one of Ms. Searle's colleagues.

When Mrs. Jay visited Mr. Liam's YouTube channel the next day, she noticed professional videos he had made as well as a link to his professional website. While visiting his website, she clicked on a link that led her to LiveBinders, a cloud-based tool she had never used before. After some exploration, she decided to use a LiveBinder to curate and organize the information she wanted to present during the inservice.

She noticed that Mr. Liam had created a LiveBinder specific to the CCSS. She e-mailed him and asked if he would help her create an electronic binder in preparation for her school's inservice. She was pleased when he agreed and spent an hour via Skype walking her through the process of creating a binder. Although the web-based tool was intuitive, the process was a challenge: she needed to learn to use the tool itself, determine which websites and documents to include within the binder, and organize the curated information within the binder's tabs. For example, she had found a collection of short video presentations discussing the CCSS for ELA on the James B. Hunt, Jr. Institute for Educational Leadership and Policy's website (www. hunt-institute.org) that she wanted to show during the inservice. In her electronic binder, she created a tab titled "Videos and Webinars" and, within that tab, a subtab for each of the three video presentations she wanted to include and added a textual description of each video's key message. She continued to work on her LiveBinder's content for a few more evenings, contacting Mr. Liam and Ms. Searle when she needed additional help.

About one week before the inservice, she decided it was time to generate a PowerPoint presentation that she would use on the day of the training as well as archive in the electronic binder for teachers to revisit when they wished. She worked on the presentation for two consecutive evenings and then tested it out on her husband. After her presentation, he asked if she had considered using Prezi, which viewers often find more visually appealing than PowerPoint. She replied that although she was familiar with the software, she found Prezi difficult to use. She had once tried to create a presentation using Prezi and, after three unproductive hours, had decided to stick with PowerPoint, her faithful standby. Together, they visited the Prezi website and watched a video introducing a new feature enabling users to import a PowerPoint presentation into the Prezi software and make simple transitions and sizing modifications to the slideshow. In less than an hour, Mrs. Jay's presentation became a Prezi production.

The day before the inservice, Mrs. Jay shared the Prezi and LiveBinder she had created with Mr. Merritt and Mr. Sorrell. After making a few minor adjustments suggested by Mr. Merritt and Mr. Sorrell, she felt confident in presenting the information to the teachers. Her only regret was that a grant application she had written to purchase a laptop for every teacher had not yet been approved, so the meeting environment would not be as participatory as she would like it to be. The computer lab had only 20 computers, so it would be difficult to engage all 60 teachers in using the LiveBinder she had created.

Nonetheless, the inservice's content and presentation were well received. Mrs. Jay, Mr. Merritt, and Mr. Sorrell announced that they wanted the teachers to review the websites, documents, and videos in the LiveBinder over the next few weeks in preparation for collaboratively formulating the summer curriculum focus. The work in the summer would include unpacking the standards to gain deeper insight into their intent and prepare to develop appropriate lesson plans and write standards-based units of study. As they exited, teachers told Mrs. Jay that they had enjoyed the Prezi presentation as well as the content in her LiveBinder. Mr. Merritt stopped by Mrs. Jay's office later in the day and told her that he was pleased with the results of the inservice. Teachers also stopped by to ask specific questions about unpacking the standards in preparation for the summer work.

Reactions and Reflections

That evening, Mrs. Jay told her husband that she felt the inservice had gone well and that she was pleased she had challenged herself to model 21st century web-based tools and applications. She admitted that she had worried a bit that her

Prezi would be lost "in the cloud" when she was ready to present, but everything had gone smoothly, and the embedded links to the videos and additional resources in her LiveBinder had worked perfectly. Although it had been frustrating that the teachers could not actively engage with the resources she had placed in the Live-Binder, quite a few teachers told her that they were looking forward to studying the curated information in the next few weeks. During her intense preparation for the inservice, she had learned much more about the CCSS for ELA and overcome a technological learning curve. When she observed the teachers' enthusiasm, she felt all her efforts had paid off.

Before going to sleep that night, Mrs. Jay recorded her thoughts in an administrative log:

• **Technology, web-based tools, and collaboration:** The technology and web-based tools I used in the upgrade provided me with virtual access to experts as collaborators—and not one of them (except my husband) worked with me in person! My virtual team played a crucial role in the success of the inservice's content and presentation.

• **Modeling:** It was satisfying to know that some teachers learned about new web-based tools (Survey Monkey, LiveBinder, and Prezi) as a result of my presentation. I hope all of our teachers decide to use these and other web-based tools and applications authentically in their classrooms.

• **CCSS for ELA:** It is crucial for administrators to make a conscious effort to integrate technology and web-based tools if we want teachers to do the same and, ultimately, if we want students to be able to use technology and digital media strategically and capably, as stated in the ELA CCR Capacities. The next challenge for all of us is to make certain that presenters and teachers are not the only ones using technology and web-based tools; students also need to learn to use these tools to respond authentically to the demands of audience, task, and purpose.

Revisions

During the summer, the teachers and administrators carefully studied the nuances of the CCSS for ELA to determine the standards' systemic learning expectations. Unpacking the reading standards led them to begin generating a focused and coherent K–12 reading curriculum. The teachers frequently used the LiveBinder that

Mrs. Jay had created and began to add tabs and subtabs of their own to extend its application. Many teachers created their own LiveBinders, some for professional learning and others for instructional purposes.

Later in the summer, the grant for the laptops was approved. The three administrators and many of the teachers were excited about the potential for developing more interactive learning and teaching opportunities and web-based inservices.

Discussion Questions

1. Mrs. Jay initially thought she would develop the inservice solo, but she ended up involving several orbits of ability (Ms. Searle, Mr. Liam, and Mr. Jay). Two of her three collaborators were not present physically. How often do you assemble a virtual team when you develop inservices or trainings? How might you locate orbits of ability you need to upgrade a current training or inservice? What could you do to offer your own orbits of ability to others?

2. Administrators who expect teachers to be intentional about 21st century instructional practices need to model those intentions themselves. If you were responsible for upgrading a professional development training or inservice, whose orbits of ability would you seek out to ensure that the training represented what you were asking of teachers?

3. Creating 21st century learning environments is not an option; it's an imperative. How might upgrading curriculum and professional development one unit at a time transform your district or school's cultural norms regarding modern learning? How might you foster collegial professional relationships, both in person and virtually?

Part III

Transformational
Reflections

There is much to contemplate when going about the business of turning classrooms, schools, and districts into living and breathing 21st century learning environments. Although it is important to be aware of anything that could influence a transformation, not every influence necessarily needs to be incorporated into every upgraded unit of study.

Jeanne Tribuzzi is a national curriculum mapping consultant, a leader in English language arts literacy, and one of our Curriculum 21 colleagues. When her audiences appear to be overwhelmed by monumental curriculum design and upgrade tasks, she shares an insight she gleaned from a vignette in Anne Lamott's (1994) book *Bird By Bird: Some Instructions on Writing and Life*:

> Thirty years ago, my older brother, who was ten years old at the time, was trying to get a report on birds written that he'd had three months to write, which was due the next day. We were out at our family cabin in Bolinas, and he was at the kitchen table close to tears, surrounded by binder paper and pencils and unopened books on birds, immobilized by the hugeness of the task ahead. Then my father sat down beside him, put his arm around my brother's shoulder, and said, "Bird by bird, buddy. Just take it bird by bird." (pp. 18–19)

The purpose of upgrading one lesson or unit at a time is to afford teachers ongoing opportunities to make strategic modifications to curriculum that help make students' learning experiences the best they can be, day by day and year by year.

Treating transformation as a gradual, collaborative process leads to meaningful and engaging learning.

The final section of this book includes two reflection chapters—one by Janet (Chapter 14) and one by Mike (Chapter 15). We hope our thoughts add to yours as you individually and collaboratively reflect on what you have gained from reading this book and as you begin transforming your curriculum "bird by bird."

14

A High School Student's Perspective

If speaking is silver, then listening is gold.

—Turkish proverb

Mike and I conducted a two-day workshop at a K–12 school to work with its teachers on upgrading units of study. Because of the school's remote location, we were asked if we would be willing to stay in two different teachers' homes. We agreed, and looked forward to meeting the teachers and their families.

The teacher with whom Mike stayed had a son, Zachary, who was in the school's senior class. During dinner, Mike explained to Zachary the concept of transforming curriculum and the importance of authentically incorporating technology and web-based tools. Zachary mentioned that as the final assessment for a unit on Greek tragedies, his English teacher had had students create PowerPoint presentations conveying what they had learned.

Later that evening, I visited Mike at Zachary's home. After making the introductions, Mike related what he and Zachary had been discussing. I asked Zachary if he would show us his PowerPoint presentation and tell us a little about the project. He assented and opened the presentation on his laptop. It was titled "Prometheus Bound." He explained that his teacher had divided the class into small groups of four or five students, and each group was responsible for creating a media presentation. He added that he was pretty sure the reason they had been assigned a PowerPoint was that all the teachers were now required to use technology in their classrooms. In previous years, students' Greek tragedy presentations had consisted of oral reports and display boards.

After Zachary had presented about half of the slides, I asked him if the entire presentation focused on retelling the tragedy and explaining a few vocabulary words and ancillary points. Zachary responded that it did, and explained that this was what the teacher had asked for. He told us that his group had done well overall but received an *A−* because its presentation had not mentioned the importance of the chorus's role in Greek theatrical dramas.

Mike asked Zachary what the unit had focused on before the final assessment. Zachary replied that the class had studied the lives and major works of three Greek playwrights—Aeschylus, Sophocles, and Euripedes—and learned about Greek drama production in the 4th and 5th centuries B.C. Throughout the unit, they answered questions posed by the teacher, either in class discussions or in quizzes.

I asked Zachary if he thought the unit would have been more engaging if it had focused on a theme, such as love, conflict, or betrayal. The students could have used the theme to draw comparisons between characters or occurrences in the Greek tragedy and current-day people or events. Zachary was not sure what I meant and asked me to clarify. I explained that when I was listening to him present "Prometheus Bound," my mind drew a correlation between Zeus's bizarre behavior of tying Prometheus to a rock and allowing an eagle to perpetually eat his liver and the recent outlandish behavior exhibited by the actor Charlie Sheen. As I saw it, the common theme was betrayal: both Zeus and Charlie Sheen had felt betrayed and reacted explosively. We discussed my reasoning for a few minutes. Zachary said he "got it." With a sparkle in his eye, he began to think of more examples of parallels between characters and plots in Greek tragedies and present-day people and events. He concluded that incorporating a theme into the unit would definitely have made creating, delivering, and listening to the Greek tragedy presentations more meaningful and interesting.

About one year later, when Mike and I were writing this book, we thought Zachary's teacher's outform upgrade—requiring students to use PowerPoint while administering the same cognitive assessment to students—might make a worthwhile snapshot to include. Because Mike and I had not worked with Zachary's teacher while we were at the school, I set up a videoconference with Zachary to ask him some preliminary questions.

I began by asking him to remind me of the specifics of the unit of study. About 10 minutes into our conversation, I realized that capturing a few moments of our dialogue would be more worthwhile for readers than creating a snapshot. The following exchange conveys a student's perception of being a passive learner versus an active learner.

Janet: Last year, when you shared your "Prometheus Bound" PowerPoint presentation with Mike and me, we discussed how the unit could have been more engaging for you and your classmates. You had mentioned that your group had done more than most. Can you give me a little background on the assignment to jog my memory?

Zachary: We were instructed to work in groups and were allowed to organize ourselves however we'd like. Since we were already divided into small groups by tables, the students at my table decided to stay together. Our teacher then assigned each group a Greek tragedy to present to the class.

Janet: Was there a reason why each group did not get to choose which Greek tragedy it would present?

Zachary: Hmmm . . . good question. We never gave it much thought, since our teachers almost always gave us our assignments. I think if we had been able to choose the Greek tragedy, we would have gone with a different one. I also think some of the students would have definitely been more involved. I have to admit I lucked out at my table. My entire group participated equally in creating our PowerPoint presentation. That was not the case for every group. I remember some students were just trying to get by and get the project done.

Janet: Are you basing that observation on what you saw taking place in the classroom?

Zachary: Sort of, but it was more than that. When my group first got started, we were really lacking direction. I decided to take on the role of being our group's leader. I delegated different tasks to everyone: several people were in charge of researching key terms presented in the tragedy, while others looked for relevant images to include in the PowerPoint. One person was in charge of writing the script that would go along with each slide. I was in charge of assembling the PowerPoint with transitions and sounds and presenting it in front of the class. We worked collaboratively to go over the presentation and make sure that everything we collectively did was properly in place. Our teacher had only required the presentation to hit a few key points about the tragedy and Greek theater, but our group went beyond everyone's expectations. I'm not trying to boast, but our presentation conveyed that our group strived for quality. It also helped that I was tech-savvy and that everyone carried his or her own weight and equally contributed to our final product.

Janet: I shared the idea of using a theme as a catalyst for learning in the unit. Do you remember that?

Zachary: Yes. It really stuck with me. Ever since then, when I am watching popular media or the news, I think of different themes, and many of them connect back to the Greek tragedies. In my college freshman English class, we have been reading Greek comedies, and I have found that some of the themes we discussed relate to the comedies as well.

Janet: It is important that students make connections to the real world as well as within and across subjects during their school years.

Zachary: I remember you and Mike talking about this. Can you remind me of what you mean exactly by "making connections"?

Janet: What unit came after the Greek tragedies unit?

Zachary: It was the final unit of the year, a senior research paper. This paper was one of two times during the year when we were allowed to pick our own topic, as long as the paper was 10 pages long and written as a formal argument. I chose to write about high-fructose corn syrup in foods marketed for children.

Janet: Let's say your English class had explored four universal themes—such as *order versus chaos, power, conflict,* and *relationships*—throughout the year. If your teacher had asked you to write a senior paper based on a self-selected theme used during the year and argue connections between what you had learned and what you would be learning after high school, it might have helped you to reflect on how universal themes are always with us. The paper could still have been written as an argument and required research.

Zachary: [quiet for a few moments] That would have been awesome, and it would have made more sense than writing about corn syrup! My education has felt so compartmentalized. What we learned in one unit was never touched on again in another unit. Making connections in one class, or, like you mentioned, between classes, is something I had never thought about before since I was never asked to think this way.

As I reflected on the Turkish proverb at the beginning of this chapter, I realized that listening closely to Zachary's thoughts and perceptions had been worth its weight in gold. Students are precious treasures waiting—and wanting—to be heard. How often do you and your colleagues listen to your students' voices? How often do you use insights gleaned from students' perceptions to upgrade learning and teaching opportunities?

15

More Than Meets the Eye

Like us, there's more to them than meets the eye.

—Optimus Prime

When Janet and I were talking about how to conclude this book, the hardest part was figuring out how to best reiterate that there is never an end to curriculum transformation. Transforming curriculum means continually upgrading existing units of study to accord with modern learning, which never stops evolving.

I shared with Janet an experience I had in an elementary school not too long ago while working with teachers on technology integration. During our lunch break, I sat at a table with Mrs. Burnett and Mrs. Gunnels, who were close friends as well as colleagues. Mrs. Burnett discussed her plans for her son's upcoming 6th birthday party. As a fan of the *Transformers* movie and television cartoons, he had requested a Transformers theme. During a recent trip to the toy store, he had asked for a Level 3 Transformers toy. Mrs. Gunnels, whose son was about the same age, shook her head and said that a Level 3 toy would be too difficult for Mrs. Burnett's son to assemble.

At this point, I chimed in. I mentioned that although I had watched all of the *Transformers* movies, my young daughter was not a fan, so I didn't understand all this talk of levels. Mrs. Burnett explained that the three different levels of Transformers toys reflected varying levels of complexity:

- **Level 1: Easy.** With a simple twist and snap, the car or machine is transformed into an Autobot (a good guy) or a Decepticon (a bad guy). Level 1 toys have the fewest moving parts and convert with a relatively simple series of steps.

- **Level 2: Intermediate.** Level 2 toys have more moving parts than Level 1 toys, and conversion requires a longer series of steps. It requires some thought to figure out how all the parts fit in the transformation.
- **Level 3: Advanced.** Level 3 toys have the most moving parts and the longest series of conversion steps. It requires much more thought to manipulate the intricate parts and transform the machine into a robot. A child who is not ready for this level may end up breaking the toy within minutes of taking it out of the box.

I was curious to know a bit more about the levels. While I was waiting for my flight at the airport later that day, I did some online investigating and found something interesting: there were currently 87 Level 1 toys, 57 Level 2 toys, and only 5 Level 3 toys on the market.

These numbers gave me a mental picture of the different levels of curriculum transformation. The largest number of teachers, who are just getting started with upgrading units of study, would likely be most comfortable attempting a Level 1 transformation. I would classify the Science in the Cloud upgrade and the Flat Stanley upgrade as Level 1 transformations. In the Flat Stanley unit, Mrs. Cohen and Mrs. Taylor were able to make just a few twists and turns to create a 21st century learning experience for their 1st graders.

Creating a Level 2 or Level 3 transformation tends to be a longer, more complex process. For that reason, it is less likely that teachers would choose to begin at these levels. I would categorize the Pinterest Art Critiques upgrade as a Level 2 transformation and the Film Festival upgrade as a Level 3 transformation. Although the online art critiques required time and effort of both teachers and students, the screenplay-writing and film production unit went to another level. Mr. Nations and Mrs. Keeley dedicated an extraordinary amount of time and effort to designing, planning, and co-teaching the upgraded unit and ensured that their students truly owned their own learning, from writing screenplays to producing films and showcasing the films for the community.

Regardless of which transformation level teachers choose, the most important impetus for upgrading units is to create 21st century learning environments that authentically incorporate technology and web-based tools, foster students' ownership of their learning, and prepare students for college and careers. The Free Dictionary (2012) defines *transformation* as "a marked change, as in appearance or character, usually for the better." Transformation *for the better* is the premise of this book and the reason Janet and I wrote it.

In the *Transformers* film (Bay, 2007), Optimus Prime, the leader of the Autobots, observed, "There's more to them than meets the eye" as he pondered how amazing human beings are. We think teachers are amazing and ready to transform. There are, of course, challenges in designing modern learning, but we believe that teachers desire to change and grow, especially when they can rely on one another's orbits of ability.

When seasoned Autobot Ironhide was tasked with diverting a flood before it destroyed people's lives and land, he exhorted his fellow robots to "Stop talkin', tighten your shock absorbers, and get in. We're gonna make a new river!" (Bloom & Gibbs, 1984).

We hope what we shared throughout this book inspires you to collaboratively create new rivers, or shape current ones, to ensure a modern environment—for your current students, and for generations to come.

Appendix:
TECHformational Matrices

Each TECHformational matrix in the Appendix visually displays how using a particular technology or web-based tool in each upgrade zone influences student learning and engagement. We have divided the 12 matrices into three categories: *digital devices*, *web-based tools*, and *curations*.

Digital Devices

Digital devices are technology hardware. We do not mention specific brand names because the important part is not the devices themselves but rather their meaningful use from a student-centered perspective. In this category, we provide matrices for digital cameras (Figure A.1), web-enabled e-reading devices (Figure A.2), and applications (apps) on digital devices (Figure A.3).

Web-Based Tools

Web-based tools are software and applications accessible via the Internet. In this category, we provide matrices for digital storytelling (Figure A.4), blogging (Figure A.5), technology- and web-based data visualization (Figure A.6), iTunes (Figure A.7), and quick response (QR) codes (Figure A.8).

Curations

Curations are collections of information assembled by students with attention to task, purpose, and audience, using technology and web-based tools. In this category, we provide matrices for e-Portfolios (Figure A.9), digital video learning libraries (Figure A.10), web-based curation (Figure A.11), and cloud-based resource management (Figure A.12).

Spark Conversations

Teachers and administrators find the TECHformational matrices useful for sparking collaborative conversations focused on student learning. A curriculum director or professional development facilitator might choose to use the matrices while posing such thought-provoking questions as

  • If I find that I spend most of my instructional time in the *conform* upgrade zone, does that indicate that I am not a quality teacher?
  • What does it mean to be *transformational* about instruction and assessment?
  • Which current units of study encourage students to *outform, reform,* or *transform*? Support your responses with evidence.
  • Does the 21st century workforce need students who can *outform, reform,* or *transform*? Cite an example from a local employer to support your reasoning.

The TECHformational matrices can be downloaded at www.ascd.org/ASCD/pdf/books/halefisherappendix2013.pdf. Use the password "hale112014" to unlock the PDF.

FIGURE

A.1 TECHformational Matrix: Digital Cameras (Digital Devices)

Impact on Learning (vertical axis)

Reform
Students analyze teacher's, peers', or own captured images/video for intended task/purpose/audience.

Transform
Students analyze intended task/purpose/audience prior to capturing images/video and edit/revise initial versions based on personal and peer feedback. Amplify, if appropriate.

Conform
Teacher uses digital camera to capture classroom and school events.

Outform
Students use camera to capture classroom and school events.

Impact on Engagement (horizontal axis)

FIGURE

A.2 TECHformational Matrix: Web-Enabled e-Reading Devices (Digital Devices)

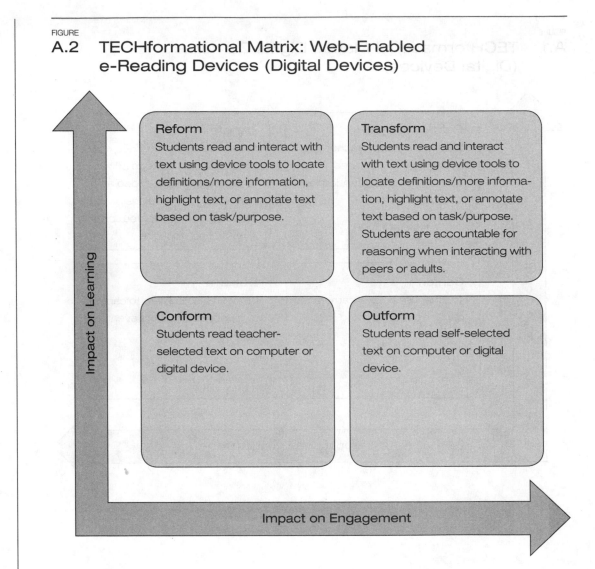

Reform
Students read and interact with text using device tools to locate definitions/more information, highlight text, or annotate text based on task/purpose.

Transform
Students read and interact with text using device tools to locate definitions/more information, highlight text, or annotate text based on task/purpose. Students are accountable for reasoning when interacting with peers or adults.

Conform
Students read teacher-selected text on computer or digital device.

Outform
Students read self-selected text on computer or digital device.

Impact on Learning

Impact on Engagement

A.3 TECHformational Matrix: Applications (Apps) on Digital Devices (Digital Devices)

Reform
Students choose appropriate apps for specific task to engage in deep, purposeful learning.

Transform
Students use existing apps and/or web-based tools to create original apps for a specific task/purpose/audience. Amplify, if appropriate.

Conform
Students use teacher-selected apps primarily for novelty or enrichment.

Outform
Students use self-selected apps primarily for novelty or enrichment.

Impact on Learning

Impact on Engagement

A.4 TECHformational Matrix: Digital Storytelling (Web-Based Tools)

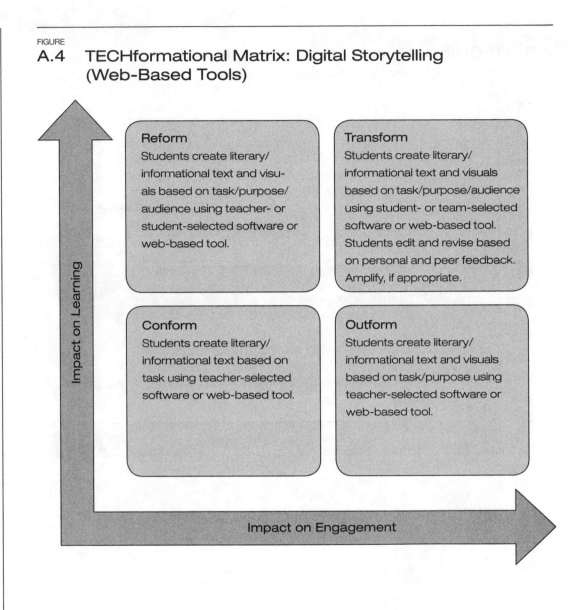

Impact on Learning

Reform
Students create literary/informational text and visuals based on task/purpose/audience using teacher- or student-selected software or web-based tool.

Transform
Students create literary/informational text and visuals based on task/purpose/audience using student- or team-selected software or web-based tool. Students edit and revise based on personal and peer feedback. Amplify, if appropriate.

Conform
Students create literary/informational text based on task using teacher-selected software or web-based tool.

Outform
Students create literary/informational text and visuals based on task/purpose using teacher-selected software or web-based tool.

Impact on Engagement

FIGURE
A.5   TECHformational Matrix: Blogging (Web-Based Tools)

Impact on Learning (vertical axis)

Reform
Students write blog posts and thoughtfully comment on other students' blog posts.

Transform
Students write blog posts and thoughtfully comment on other students' blog posts. Students revise and edit their blog posts based on peer comments.

Conform
Students write blog posts on a teacher-created blog based on task/purpose/audience.

Outform
Students supplement their blog posts with pictures and hyperlinks.

Impact on Engagement (horizontal axis)

FIGURE
A.6 TECHformational Matrix: Technology- and Web-Based Data Visualization (Web-Based Tools)

Reform

Students make creative decisions about the visualization of self-selected data collection based on task/purpose/audience using their choice of software or web-based tool.

Transform

Students choose software or web-based tool to create visualizations based on task/purpose/audience that represent their collected and curated data. Amplify, if appropriate.

Conform

Students use word-processing, spreadsheet, presentation, or graphic design software to contribute to or interact with teacher-created graphs, charts, or displays.

Outform

Students make creative decisions about the visualization of teacher-selected data using their choice of software or web-based tool.

Impact on Learning

Impact on Engagement

A.7 TECHformational Matrix: iTunes (Web-Based Tools)

Reform
Students develop and defend rationale for relevancy of self-selected iTunes U or podcasts for learning.

Transform
Students create audio/video content based on task/purpose/audience. Students contribute to iTunes for global access.

Conform
Teacher finds relevant content through iTunes U or podcasts for instructional use.

Outform
Students find relevant content through iTunes U or podcasts based on teacher guidelines to aid learning.

Impact on Learning

Impact on Engagement

FIGURE
A.8   TECHformational Matrix: Quick Response (QR) Codes (Web-Based Tools)

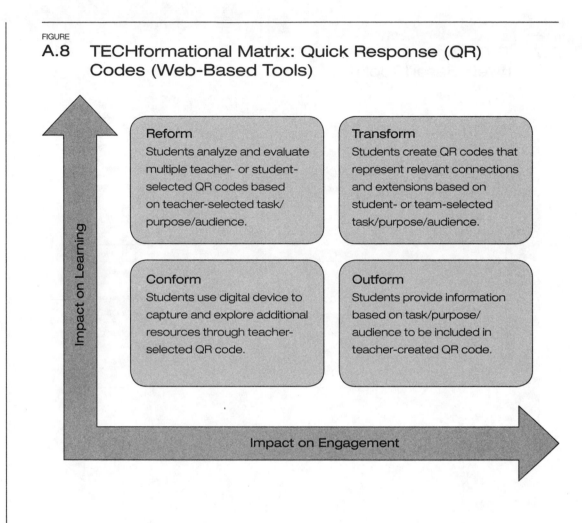

Reform
Students analyze and evaluate multiple teacher- or student-selected QR codes based on teacher-selected task/purpose/audience.

Transform
Students create QR codes that represent relevant connections and extensions based on student- or team-selected task/purpose/audience.

Conform
Students use digital device to capture and explore additional resources through teacher-selected QR code.

Outform
Students provide information based on task/purpose/audience to be included in teacher-created QR code.

Impact on Learning

Impact on Engagement

FIGURE
A.9 TECHformational Matrix: e-Portfolios (Curations)

Reform
Student-selected textual/audio/video personal work samples are archived in teacher- or school-selected electronic/web-based tool based on task/purpose. Students improve submissions based on teacher feedback on samples.

Transform
Student-selected textual/audio/video personal work samples are archived in student-, teacher-, or school-selected electronic/web-based tool based on ongoing task/purpose. Students improve submissions based on teacher and peer feedback on samples.

Conform
Teacher-selected textual/audio/video student work samples are archived in teacher- or school-selected electronic/web-based tool.

Outform
Teacher- or student-selected textual/audio/video personal work samples are archived in teacher- or school-selected electronic/web-based tool.

Impact on Learning

Impact on Engagement

FIGURE
A.10 TECHformational Matrix: Digital Video Learning Libraries (Curations)

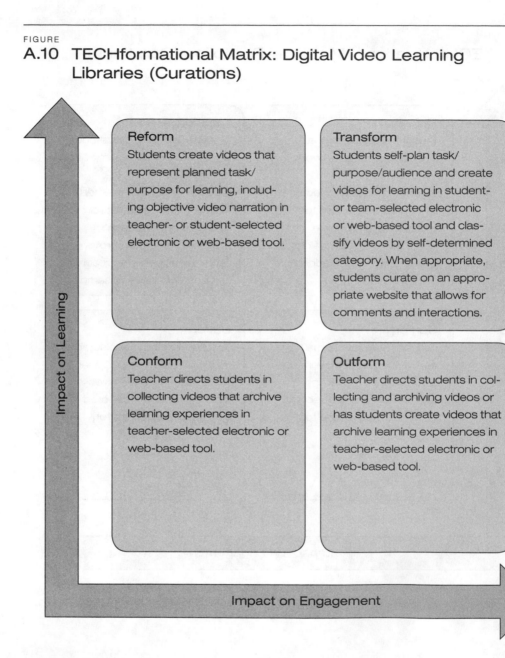

Reform
Students create videos that represent planned task/purpose for learning, including objective video narration in teacher- or student-selected electronic or web-based tool.

Transform
Students self-plan task/purpose/audience and create videos for learning in student- or team-selected electronic or web-based tool and classify videos by self-determined category. When appropriate, students curate on an appropriate website that allows for comments and interactions.

Conform
Teacher directs students in collecting videos that archive learning experiences in teacher-selected electronic or web-based tool.

Outform
Teacher directs students in collecting and archiving videos or has students create videos that archive learning experiences in teacher-selected electronic or web-based tool.

Impact on Learning

Impact on Engagement

FIGURE

A.11 TECHformational Matrix: Web-Based Curation (Curations)

Impact on Learning (vertical axis)

Reform
Students curate and annotate teacher-selected multimedia based on task/purpose/ audience according to teacher- or student-defined curation parameters in teacher- or student-selected web-based tool.

Transform
Students choose web-based tools to collect, curate, and annotate multimedia based on task/purpose/audience and provide reasoning for the content's inclusion. Amplify, if appropriate.

Conform
During instruction, students view multimedia curated by the teacher based on task/ purpose in teacher-selected web-based tool.

Outform
Students curate teacher-selected multimedia based on task/purpose in teacher-selected web-based tool.

Impact on Engagement (horizontal axis)

163

FIGURE
A.12 TECHformational Matrix: Cloud-Based Resource Management (Curations)

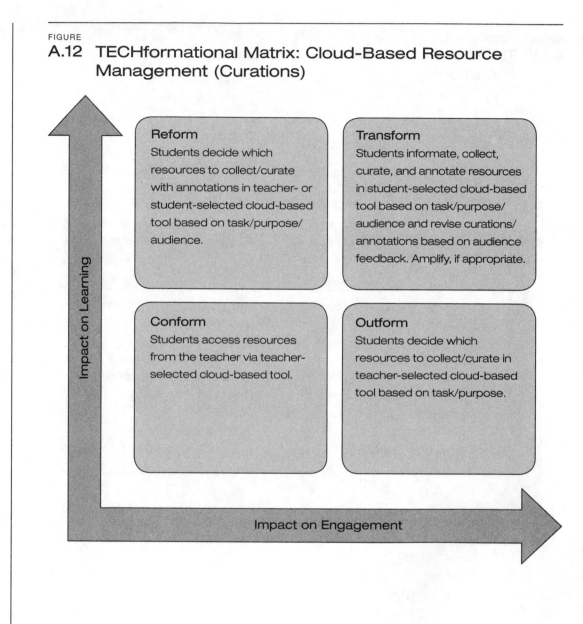

Reform
Students decide which resources to collect/curate with annotations in teacher- or student-selected cloud-based tool based on task/purpose/audience.

Transform
Students informate, collect, curate, and annotate resources in student-selected cloud-based tool based on task/purpose/audience and revise curations/annotations based on audience feedback. Amplify, if appropriate.

Conform
Students access resources from the teacher via teacher-selected cloud-based tool.

Outform
Students decide which resources to collect/curate in teacher-selected cloud-based tool based on task/purpose.

Impact on Learning

Impact on Engagement

References

Bach, R. (n.d.). Richard Bach quote. Retrieved May 28, 2012, from www.inspirational stories.com/quotes/t/richard-bach/page/2

Bay, M. (Director). (2007). *Transformers* [Motion picture]. United States: Paramount Pictures.

Bloom, G. A. (Writer), & Gibbs, J. (Director). (1984, September 19). More than meets the eye: Part 3. *The Transformers* [Television series]. Japan: Toei Animation Co. Ltd.

Brown, J. (1964). *Flat Stanley*. London: HarperCollins.

Busteed, B. (2012, May 23). In education, technology changes everything and nothing. HuffingtonPost Blog. Retrieved from www.huffingtonpost.com/brandon-busteed/technology-in-classrooms_b_1541020.html?ref=technology&ir=Technology

Costa, A. L., & Kallick, B. (1995). *Assessment in the learning organization: Shifting the paradigm*. Alexandria, VA: ASCD.

Darling-Hammond, L. (1997). *The right to learn: A blueprint for creating schools that work*. San Francisco: Jossey-Bass.

de Stael, Mme. (n.d.). Madame de Stael quote. Retrieved May 28, 2012, from www.brainyquote.com/quotes/quotes/m/madamedest145776.html

DuFour, R., Eaker, R., & DuFour, R. (2005). *On common ground: The power of professional learning communities*. Bloomington, IN: National Educational Service.

Edutopia. (2011). *Top ten tips for assessing project-based learning*. Retrieved May 28, 2012, from www.edutopia.org/10-tips-assessment-project-based-learning-resource-guide/

Go-Gulf. (2011, June 1). 60 seconds: Things that happen on Internet every sixty seconds [blog post]. Retrieved from www.go-gulf.com/blog/60-seconds

Hale, J. A., & Dunlap, R. F. (2010). *An educational leader's guide to curriculum mapping: Creating and sustaining collaborative cultures*. Thousand Oaks, CA: Corwin Press.

Hos-McGrane, M. (2010, April 19). The SAMR model: From theory to practice [blog post]. *Tech Transformation* blog post. Retrieved from *Tech Transformation* at www.maggiehosmcgrane.com/2010/04/samr-model-from-theory-to-practice.html

Jacobs, H. H. (2002). Integrated curriculum design. In J. Y. Klein (Ed.), *Interdisciplinary education K–12 and college: A foundation for K–16 dialogue* (pp. 23–44). New York: College Board.

Jacobs, H. H. (2010). *Curriculum 21: Essential education for a changing world.* Alexandria, VA: ASCD.

Jacobs, H. H. (2011). Keynote presentation at the Seventeenth National Curriculum Mapping Institute, Saratoga Springs, New York.

Jensen, J. (2011, June 17). Kids at heart: J. J. Abrams and Steven Spielberg swap stories about their wide-eyed beginnings, their lifelong obsessions, and listening to their inner children on the set of *Super 8. Entertainment Weekly*, 64–72.

Keller, H. (n.d.). Helen Keller quote. Retrieved May 28, 2012, from www.brainyquote.com/quotes/quotes/h/helenkelle382259.html

Kennedy, J. F. (n.d.). John F. Kennedy quote. Retrieved May 28, 2012, from www.brainyquote.com/quotes/quotes/j/johnfkenn110084.html

Kiva. (n.d.). About microfinance. Retrieved May 28, 2012, from www.kiva.org/about/microfinance

Lamott, A. (1994). *Bird by bird: Some instructions on writing and life.* New York: Doubleday.

Laufenberg, D. (2010). *How to learn? From mistakes.* TEDx Talk transcript. Retrieved May 28, 2012, from http://dotsub.com/view/19e719b2-e3f8-482b-bfd7-55165bca949d/viewTranscript/eng

Lynch, L. (2011, July 12). *Digital learning: Final chapter for textbooks?* Retrieved May 28, 2012, from www.schools.com/visuals/digital-learning-final-chapter-for-textbooks.html

Marzano, R. J. (2007). *The art and science of teaching: A comprehensive framework for effective instruction.* Alexandria, VA: ASCD.

Mead, M. (n.d.). Margaret Mead quote. Retrieved May 28, 2012, from http://thinkexist.com/quotes/margaret_mead/2.html

National Governors Association Center for Best Practices (NGA Center) & Council of Chief State School Officers (CCSSO). (2010a). *Common Core State Standards for English Language Arts and Literacy in History/Social Studies, Science, and Technical Subjects.* Washington, DC: Author.

National Governors Association Center for Best Practices (NGA Center) & Council of Chief State School Officers (CCSSO). (2010b). *Common Core State Standards for Mathematics.* Washington, DC: Author.

November, A. (2010). *Empowering students with technology* (2nd ed.). Thousand Oaks, CA: Corwin Press.

November, A. (2012). *Who owns the learning? Preparing students for success in the digital age.* Bloomington, IN: Solution Tree Press.

Partnership for 21st Century Skills. (2009). *Framework for 21st century learning.* Retrieved May 28, 2012, from www.p21.org/index.php?option=com_content&task=view&id=254&Itemid=120

Puentedura, R. (2011). *SAMR and change.* Retrieved May 28, 2012, from www.hippasus.com/rrpweblog/archives/2011/10/27/SAMR_And_Change.pdf

Rosenthal Tolisano, S. (2011a, August 8). The next step: Amplification . . . amplify. . . . [blog post]. Retrieved from *Langwitches Blog* at http://langwitches.org/blog/2011/08/08/the-next-step-amplification-amplify

Rosenthal Tolisano, S. (2011b, July 21). Upgrade your KWL chart to the 21st century [blog post]. Retrieved from *Langwitches Blog* at http://langwitches.org/blog/2011/07/21/upgrade-your-kwl-chart-to-the-21st-century

Schuch, S. (2002). *A symphony of whales.* Boston: Sandpiper.

Scieszka, J. (1996). *The true story of the three little pigs.* New York: Puffin.

Shocking education statistics. (2010). *Lessons in Education.* Retrieved May 28, 2012, from www.oprah.com/relationships/Shocking-Education-Statistics

Stewart, V. (2012). *A world-class education: Learning from international models of excellence and innovation.* Alexandria, VA: ASCD.

Turkish proverb. (n.d.). Turkish proverb. Retrieved May 28, 2012, from www.leadershipnow.com/listeningquotes.html

Wang, V. (n.d.). Vera Wang quote. Retrieved May 28, 2012, from www.brainyquote.com/quotes/quotes/v/verawang272302.html

Wiggins, G., & McTighe, J. (2005). *Understanding by design* (Expanded 2nd ed.). Alexandria, VA: ASCD.

Wiggins, G., & McTighe, J. (2011). *The Understanding by Design guide to creating high-quality units.* Alexandria, VA: ASCD.

Young, E. (1989). *Lon po po.* New York: Philomel.

Index

The letter *f* following a page number denotes a figure.

Abrams, J. J., 9
Adobe InDesign, 129
Amazon.com, 117, 118
amplifying tasks, 33, 37
analysis and evaluation skills, 131
appraising and brainstorming phase, 41–42. *See also specific snapshots*
apps, 20, 155*f*
architects, teachers as, 15
argumentative writing skills, 132
arguments, constructing, 81*f*, 88
Around the World with 80 Schools, 90
ASCD Edge, 5, 11, 48
ASCD Twitter hashtag, 37
augmentation automating tasks, 33, 35
augmentation upgrade, automating, 28–29, 28*f*
automating
    augmentation upgrade, 28–29, 28*f*
    informating vs., 29
    SAMR Continuum model, 28*f*
    substitution upgrade, 27–28, 28f
automating-informating-amplifying continuum, 27, 28*f*

backchanneling, 36*f*, 37–38
Bird By Bird (Lamott), 141
blogs, 65, 67, 106–109, 111–114
Into the Book, 64
Box, 117

Children's Internet Protection Act (CIPA), 128, 129, 131
clarifications. *See also specific clarification skills*
    collaboration, 22
    glocal-impact units, 23–24
    higher-order thinking, 21–22
    local and global connections, 22–23
cloud-based resource management, 164*f*
cloud computing, 117, 137. *See also* Science in the Cloud (snapshot)
collaboration
    amplifying for, 31–33
    CCSS requirement, 2, 11
    Internet-based, 11–12
    orbits of ability component, 10–11, 10*f*
    technology and web-based tools for, 22–23
    transforming requirement of, 9–10
collaboration skills
    Flat Stanley podcast, 66
    glocal-impact units, 24
    a high school student's perspective, 143–147
    Microloans, 87
    Professional Development, CCSS inservice, 139
    Science in the Cloud, 121
    Social Justice Live! 113
    ten-frame mathematics lesson plan, 58–59
    21st century requirement for, 2, 22

collaborative environment lens
    Flat Stanley podcast, 61*f*
    Pinterest Art Critiques, 123*f*
    Professional Development, CCSS inservice, 134*f*
    Science in the Cloud, 116*f*
    Social Justice Live! 105*f*
    Talk Pals, 69*f*
    ten-frame mathematics lesson plan, 49*f*
College and Career Readiness (CCR) Capacities (CCSS for ELA). *See also specific skills*
    amplifying upgrade and, 33
    Film Festival, 91*f*
    Flat Stanley podcast, 61*f*
    Microloans, 81*f*
    Pinterest Art Critiques, 123*f*
    Professional Development, CCSS inservice, 72–73
    Science in the Cloud, 116*f*
    Social Justice Live! 105*f*
    Talk Pals, 69*f*
    21st century requirement for, 33
commitment, defined, 42
commitment and communication phase, 42–43. *See also specific snapshots*
Common Core State Standards (CCSS). *See also* Professional Development, CCSS inservice; *specific standards*
    collaboration skills in, 2, 11
    content standards, 24–25
    goal of, 24
    process-skills standards, 24–25
    upgrading, basis for, 25
communication skills, 58–59, 67, 77, 113, 131
conform zone
    backchanneling in the, 36*f*, 37
    curations and the, 161–164*f*
    digital devices and the, 153–155*f*
    impact on learning and engagement, 12
    interactive whiteboards in the, 35, 35*f*
    substitution upgrade and, 28
    web-based tools and the, 156–160*f*
content knowlege, building, 81*f*
contractors, teachers as, 15
critical thinking skills. *See also* Pinterest Art Critiques (snapshot)
    Film Festival, 91*f*
    Flat Stanley podcast, 66
    Microloans, 81*f*, 87, 88
    Social Justice Live! 105*f*
    ten-frame mathematics lesson plan, 58
culminating experiences
    Film Festival, 91*f*
    Flat Stanley podcast, 19, 61*f*
    overview, 19

curations
    cloud-based resource management, 164*f*
    defined, 152
    digital video learning libraries, 162*f*
    e-Portfolios, 161*f*
    web-based, 163*f*
curriculum, transforming the. *See also* enhancement-transformation continuum
    collaboration in, 2, 9–10
    a high school student's perspective, 143–147
    levels of, 149
    online resources, 5
    orbits of ability , 10–11, 10*f*
    performance task assessments for, 17–19
    process of, 141–142
    purpose of, 149
    requirements, Jacobs on, 2
    spiral of transformation, 40–44
    21st Century (teacher) Pledge, 34
curriculum examinations
    Film Festival, 91*f*
    Microloans, 81*f*
    overview, 19–20
    Pinterest Art Critiques, 123*f*
    Social Justice Live! 105*f*
    Talk Pals, 69*f*
    technology and web-based tools for, 20

data visualization, 158*f*
digital cameras, 153*f*
digital devices
    apps on, 155*f*
    defined, 151
    digital cameras, 153*f*
    using, standards requirement for, 69*f*, 81*f*, 88, 91*f*, 113, 116*f*, 121, 123*f*, 131
    web-enabled e-reading devices, 154*f*
digital learning farm model, 25
digital learning networks (DLNs)
    accessing orbits of ability with, 11–12
    ASCD Edge, 5, 11, 48
    online resources, 11
    Social Justice Live! 106, 107, 110
    on Twitter, 11–12, 70–71, 82, 83, 106
digital storytelling, 67, 156*f*
digital video learning libraries, 162*f*
Diigo, 11
Dropbox, 117–121

ELA Essential Maps, 92
Empowering Students with Technology (November), 26
engagement. *See also specific zones*
    automating vs. informating, 29–30
    a high school student's perspective, 143–147
    playground tools for, 12–13
    upgrade zones impact on, 12–13, 13*f*

English Language Arts & Literacy in History/
Social Studies, Science, and Technical Subjects
(CCSS for ELA). *See also specific skills*
    CCR Capacities, 33, 61*f*, 69*f*, 72–73, 81*f*,
        91*f*, 105*f*, 116*f*, 123*f*
    expectations for modern classrooms, 11
    Film Festival, 92
    Microloans, 89
    Pinterest Art Critiques, 124, 132
    process-skills standards, 24
    Science in the Cloud, 121
    Social Justice Live! 106, 114
    Speaking and Listening, 71–79
    Talk Pals, 71–77
    technology requirements, 26–27
    ten-frame mathematics lesson plan, 50
enhancement-transformation continuum. *See also*
    curriculum, transforming the
    amplifying, 31–33
    automating, 27–30, 28*f*
    informating, 28*f*, 29–31
entry levels, 17
entry points. *See also specific points of entry*
    culminating experiences, 19
    curriculum examinations, 19–20
    instructional innovations, 20–21
    overview, 17–19
e-Portfolios, 161*f*
e-reading devices, web-enabled, 154*f*
evidence, valuing, 81*f*, 105*f*, 121, 123*f*

Facebook, 11, 20, 106, 111
Film Festival (snapshot)
    appraising and brainstorming phase, 92–93
    commitment and communication phase,
        93–101
    reactions and reflections phase, 101–103
    revisions phase, 103
    technology authenticity, 91*f*, 102–103
    transformational lenses, 91*f*
    upgrade level, 149
Flat Stanley podcast (snapshot)
    appraising and brainstorming phase,
        62–63
    reactions and reflections phase, 66–67
    revisions phase, 68
    technology authenticity, 61*f*, 67
    transformational lenses, 61*f*
    upgrade level, 149
Flickr, 132

GarageBand, 65, 67
global connections. *See also* Microloans (snapshot)
    amplifying for, 31–32
    Flat Stanley podcast, 61*f*, 65–66, 69*f*
    online resources for teachers, 90

Social Justice Live! 105*f*, 107, 113
Talk Pals, 69*f*, 70–71, 74–78
technology and web-based tools for, 22–23
21st century learning environments for, 22,
    23
glocal impacts units of study, 23–24. *See also* Micro-
    loans (snapshot)
Google Art Project, 132
Google Docs, 107, 108, 109, 110, 117, 118, 131
Google for Educators, 107
Google Forms, 107
Google Maps, 66, 67

hardware, types of, 26
higher-order thinking skills
    Film Festival, 91*f*, 102
    Flat Stanley podcast, 61*f*
    Microloans, 81*f*
    Social Justice Live! 105*f*, 112–113
    ten-frame mathematics lesson plan, 49*f*
    21st century, 21–22
    21st century requirement for, 2
high-skill jobs, future requirements for, 7

InDesign, 129
informating
    automating vs., 29
    enhancement-transformation continuum,
        29–31
    modification stage, 28*f*, 30
    redefinition stage, 28*f*, 30–31
    SAMR Continuum model, 28*f*
information, location of, 31
information literacy, 121
Institute for Educational Leadership and Policy,
    137
instructional innovation
    Film Festival, 91*f*
    Flat Stanley podcast, 61*f*
    Microloans, 81*f*
    Pinterest Art Critiques, 123*f*
    Professional Development, CCSS inservice,
        134*f*, 139
    Science in the Cloud, 116*f*
    Social Justice Live! 105*f*
    Talk Pals, 69*f*
    ten-frame mathematics lesson plan, 49*f*
interactive whiteboards
    Flat Stanley podcast, 63, 65, 67
    incorporating, TEChformational Matrix
        example, 35–37, 35*f*
    Microloans, 88
    Pinterest Art Critiques, 130
    Science in the Cloud, 119, 121
    ten-frame mathematics lesson plan, 53–58
Internet, 60-second snapshot of activity on the, 20

Internet (web-based) tools. *See also* technology and web-based tools use, standards for
    data visualization, 158*f*
    defined, 151
    digital storytelling, 156*f*
    iTunes, 159*f*
    Quick Response (QR) codes, 160*f*
    types of, 26
iPhone, 20
iTunes, 117, 118, 159*f*

Jonathan Livingston Seagull (Bach), 47

Keller, Helen, 1
Kennedy, John F., 26, 39
Kiva, 83–85, 88–90

learning. *See also specific zones*
    focus of, 15
    student-centered ownership of, 13
    upgrade zones impact on, 12–13, 13*f*
learning environments, 21st century
    CCR Capacities in, 33
    elements of, 2, 21–23
    global connections in, 22, 23
    teacher's role, 21
    workplace success, ensuring with, 11, 12, 22
listening skills, 67, 77–78
literacy
    informational, 31
    media, 67
LiveBinder, 88, 108, 109–110, 113, 137, 138–139
local connections
    collaborative environments for, 22
    Film Festival, 91*f*, 102
    Flat Stanley podcast, 68, 69*f*
    Pinterest Art Critiques, 123*f*, 131
    Social Justice Live! 105*f*, 107, 110–111, 113
    Talk Pals, 72–73
    technology and web-based tools for, 22

Mathematical Practice Standards (CCSSM)
    Microloans, 81*f*, 89
    process-skills standards, 24
    ten-frame mathematics lesson plan, 49*f*, 50–54
Mead, Margaret, 7
media literacy, 67, 69*f*, 81*f*, 88, 91*f*, 113, 116*f*, 121, 123*f*, 131
Microloans (snapshot)
    appraising and brainstorming phase, 82–83
    commitment and communication phase, 83–87
    reactions and reflections phase, 87–88
    revisions phase, 89–90
    technology authenticity, 81*f*, 88
    transformational lenses, 81*f*

modification informating tasks, 33, 38
modification stage, informating, 28*f*, 30
Museum Box, 132

ooVoo, 22, 106
Optimus Prime, 148, 150
oral fluency, 67
orbits of ability , 10–12, 10*f*
outform zone
    augmentation upgrade and, 29
    backchanneling in the, 36*f*, 37
    curations and the, 161–164*f*
    digital devices and the, 153–155*f*
    interactive whiteboards in the, 35, 35*f*
    learning and engagement, impact on, 13, 13*f*
    Professional Development, CCSS inservice, 134*f*
    Science in the Cloud, 116*f*
    Talk Pals, 69*f*
    web-based tools and the, 156–160*f*

performance skills, 81*f*, 91*f*, 102, 105*f*, 123*f*
performance task assessments
    Film Festival, 91*f*
    Microloans, 81*f*
    Pinterest Art Critiques, 123*f*
    for transforming curriculum, 17–19
Pinterest, 127–131
Pinterest Art Critiques (snapshot)
    appraising and brainstorming phase, 124–126
    commitment and communication phase, 126–130
    reactions and reflections phase, 130–132
    revisions phase, 132
    standards connections, 123*f*
    technology authenticity, 123*f*, 126–130, 131
    transformational lenses, 123*f*
    upgrade level, 149
playground tools, 12–13
podcasts, 63–66. *See also* Flat Stanley podcast (snapshot)
Prezi, 138–139
problem solving skills, 49*f*, 66
Professional Development, CCSS inservice
    appraising and brainstorming phase, 135
    CCR Capacities in the, 72–73
    commitment and communication phase, 135–138
    reactions and reflections phase, 138–139
    revisions phase, 139–140
    technology authenticity, 134*f*, 137, 139
    transformational lenses, 134*f*
professional learning community (PLC), 11
project-based learning, assessing, 17

Quick Response (QR) codes, 160*f*

reactions and reflections phase, 43–44. *See also
    specific snapshots*
reading skills, 78
reasoning skills, 49*f*, 81*f*
redefinition informating tasks, 38
redefinition stage, informating, 28*f*, 30–31
reform zone
        augmentation upgrade and, 29
        backchanneling in the, 36*f*, 38
        curations and the, 161–164*f*
        digital devices and the, 153–155*f*
        interactive whiteboards in the, 35*f*, 36
        learning and engagement, impact on,
            12–13, 13*f*
        web-based tools and the, 156–160*f*
revisions phase, 43–44. *See also specific snapshots*

SAMR Continuum model, 28*f*
Science in the Cloud (snapshot)
        appraising and brainstorming phase,
            117–118
        commitment and communication phase,
            118–120
        reactions and reflections phase, 120–122
        revisions phase, 122
        technology authenticity, 116*f*, 117–118, 121
        transformational lenses, 116*f*
        upgrade level, 149
Scribd, 20
Skype
        60-second snapshot of activity on, 20
        for local and global connections, 22, 23
        for professional development, 137
        Talk Pals, 74–75, 78
Skype in the Classroom, 90
Social Justice Live! (snapshot)
        appraising and brainstorming phase,
            106–107
        commitment and communication phase,
            107–112
        reactions and reflections phase, 112–114
        revisions phase, 114
        technology authenticity, 113
        transformational lenses, 105*f*
social networking, 11, 127–128. *See also specific types of*
software, types of, 26
speaking and listening skills, 67, 77–78
Spielberg, Steven, 9
spiral of transformation
        appraising and brainstorming phase, 41–42
        commitment and communication phase,
            42–43
        loop vs., 40
        reactions and reflections phase, 43–44
        revisions phase, 43–44

Stael, Madame de, 40
standards connections, 24–25
subitizing, 51
substitution upgrade, automating, 27–28, 28f
Survey Monkey, 135–136

Talk Pals (snapshot)
        appraising and brainstorming phase, 70–73
        commitment and communication phase,
            73–77
        reactions and reflections phase, 77–78
        revisions phase, 78–79
        technology authenticity, 69*f*
        transformational lenses, 69*f*
teachers
        21st Century (teacher) Pledge, 34
        roles of, 15, 21
Teachers Recess, 82
TECHformational matrix
        backchanneling example, 36*f*, 37–38
        curations category, 152, 161–164*f*
        digital devices category, 151, 153–155*f*
        interactive whiteboards example, 35–37,
            35*f*
        introduction, 34
        web-based tools category, 151, 158–160*f*
technology and web-based tools, integrating. *See
    also specific snapshots; specific tools and technologies*
        amplifying upgrade, 31–33
        augmentation upgrade, 28–29
        automating upgrade, 27–29
        backchanneling, 36*f*, 37–38
        in collaborative environments, 22–23
        in curriculum examinations, 20
        for global connections, 22–23
        hardware, types of, 26
        a high school student's perspective, 143–147
        informating upgrade, 29–31
        in instructional innovations, 20
        for local connections, 22
        Professional Development, CCSS inservice,
            134*f*, 137, 139
        SAMR Continuum model, 28*f*
        software, types of, 26
        substitution upgrade, 27–28
        task vs. tool focus in, 38–39
        transform upgrade vs., 34
technology and web-based tools use, standards con-
    nection. *See also* Flat Stanley podcast (snapshot)
        Film Festival, 91*f*, 102–103
        Microloans, 81*f*, 88
        Pinterest Art Critiques, 123*f*, 126–131
        Science in the Cloud, 116*f*, 117–118, 121
        Social Justice Live! 113
        Talk Pals, 69*f*
        ten-frame mathematics, lesson plan
            example, 49*f*

technology and web-based tools use, standards for. *See also specific technologies*

ten-frame mathematics, lesson plan example
    appraising and brainstorming phase, 50–51
    commitment and communication phase, 51–58
    reactions and reflections phase, 58–59
    revisions phase, 59
    standards connections, 49*f*
    technology authenticity, 49*f*
    transformational lenses, 49*f*

TodaysMeet, 88, 95, 109, 110

transformation, defined, 149

transformational lenses. *See also specific lenses; specific snapshots*
    entry levels, 17
    entry points, 17–19
    standards connections, 24–25
    synthesized, 25
    teacher roles, 15

transformational matrix upgrade zones, 12–13, 13*f*. *See also specific zones*

Transformers (movie), 148, 150

Transformers (toys), 148–149

transform zone
    backchanneling in the, 36*f*, 38
    curations and the, 161–164*f*
    digital devices and the, 153–155*f*
    interactive whiteboards in the, 35*f*, 36
    learning and engagement, impact on, 13, 13*f*
    web-based tools and the, 156–160*f*

Twitter
    60-second snapshot of activity on, 20
    backchanneling compared, 37
    digital learning networks on, 11–12, 70–71, 82, 83, 106
    Flat Stanley podcast, 67
    mentioned, 11
    Social Justice Live! 106, 111

upgrade zones impact on learning and engagement, 13*f*. *See also specific zones*

uStream, 109, 111

videoconferencing
    Microloans, 82–83, 86–87
    Professional Development, CCSS inservice, 137
    Skype for, 74–75, 78
    Social Justice Live! 106–107, 109, 110–111
    Talk Pals, 70–73, 74–77, 78

Wallwisher, 109, 110

Wang, Vera, 15

Who Do You Think You Are? 47

wikis, 12, 94–95

workplace success, ensuring, 11, 12, 22

writing skills, 67, 81*f*, 88, 132

YouTube, 20, 137

About the Authors

 **Janet A. Hale** is an educational consultant who specializes in curriculum mapping, standards-based curriculum design, and transforming units of study. She travels extensively throughout the United States as well as internationally. She enjoys introducing curriculum design and curriculum mapping to newcomers, supporting implementation, aiding struggling initiatives, and advising those ready for advanced curriculum work. She has written two books focused on curriculum mapping, including *A Guide to Curriculum Mapping: Planning, Implementing, and Sustaining the Process* and *An Educational Leader's Guide to Curriculum Mapping: Creating and Sustaining Collaborative Cultures*, both published by Corwin Press.

Her experience as a teacher at the elementary and secondary levels and her master's degree in leadership and curriculum are an asset to her work helping teachers and administrators design curriculum maps and transform units of study. Since 1988, Janet has developed national educational seminars and trainings and presented at conferences sponsored by ASCD, the International Reading Association, the Association of Christian Schools International, and Curriculum Designers/Curriculum 21.

Janet resides in Tucson, Arizona. At home, she enjoys working in her desert garden and spending time with family and friends. She may be reached at 520-241-8797 or teachtucson@aol.com. You may also visit her website at www.CurriculumMapping101.com.

Michael Fisher is an instructional coach and educational consultant specializing in the intersection between instructional technology and curriculum design, which he calls *digigogy:* a new digital pedagogy. He works with districts across the United States to help schools and educators maximize available technology, software, and web-based resources while attending to curriculum design, instructional practices, and assessments.

Michael holds a bachelor's degree in science from the University of North Carolina at Wilmington, a master's degree in English from Buffalo State College, and postbaccalaureate certifications in middle grades science, English language arts, and K–12 gifted education. He presents at local, regional, and national conferences in the United States and has also worked internationally, most recently with the first ever 1:1 iPad implementation in China. He is a frequent blogger on ASCD EDge (ascdedge.ascd.org), the Curriculum 21 Ning (curriculum21.ning.com), and his professional blog (digigogy.blogspot.com).

Michael resides in Amherst, New York. He enjoys spending time with family as well as reading and writing. He may be reached at digigogy@gmail.com or through his website (www.digigogy.com).

Related ASCD Resources:
Upgrading Curriculum and Professional Development

At the time of publication, the following ASCD resources were available (ASCD stock numbers appear in parentheses). For up-to-date information about ASCD resources, go to www.ascd.org. You can search the complete archives of *Educational Leadership* at http://www.ascd.org/el.

Professional Interest Communities
Visit the ASCD website and scroll to the bottom to click on "professional interest communities." Within these communities, find information about professional educators who have formed groups around topics like "Instructional Technology" and "Professional Learning Communities."

ASCD EDge Groups
Exchange ideas and connect with other educators interested in various topics, including Curriculum and Instruction, Curriculum Mapping, and Instructional Technology on the social networking site ASCD EDge™.

PD Online
Crafting Curriculum: An Introduction by Kathy Checkley (#PD09OC25)
Differentiated Instruction: The Curriculum Connection (#PD11OC116)
From Vision to Action: The 21st Century Teaching and Learning Plan (#PD11OC126)
Schools as Professional Learning Communities: An Introduction by Vera Blake and Diane L. Jackson (#PD09OC28)
Technology in Schools: A Balanced Perspective, 2nd Ed. (#PD11OC109)

These and other online courses are available at www.ascd.org/pdonline

Print Products
Curriculum 21: Essential Education for a Changing World by Heidi Hayes Jacobs (Ed.) (#109008)
The Curriculum Mapping Planner: Templates, Tools, and Resources for Effective Professional Development by Heidi Hayes Jacobs and Ann W. Johnson (#109010)
Getting Results with Curriculum Mapping by Heidi Hayes Jacobs (#104011)
Taking Charge of Professional Development: A Practical Model for Your School by Joseph Semadeni (#109029)

DVDs
21st Century Skills: Promoting Creativity and Innovation in the Classroom (#609096)
Curriculum Mapping: Charting the Course for Content (with facilitator's guide) (#699049)
Differentiated Instruction and Curriculum Mapping: What's the Fit? (#611019)
Getting Results with Curriculum Mapping (with facilitator's guide) (#606167)

The Whole Child Initiative
THE WHOLE CHILD The Whole Child Initiative helps schools and communities create learning environments that allow students to be healthy, safe, engaged, supported, and challenged. To learn more about other books and resources that relate to the whole child, visit www.wholechildeducation.org.

For more information: send e-mail to member@ascd.org; call 1-800-933-2723 or 703-578-9600, press 2; send a fax to 703-575-5400; or write to Information Services, ASCD, 1703 N. Beauregard St., Alexandria, VA 22311-1714 USA.